"Equal parts commentary on tl
Turner's latest book, *New Church, New Altar: A Commentary
on the Order of Dedication of a Church and an Altar*, is essential
reading for anyone building a church. It seamlessly weaves
together the various rites, their history and meaning, and the
applicable liturgical law to reveal that building a church is never
just a construction project: it is also for and about 'building up
spiritually the people of God into a dwelling place for God with
Christ Jesus himself as the cornerstone' (Eph 2:21). And if you're
not building a church, don't ignore this gem: use it to guide your
community into a mystagogical reflection on how your church
building and the rites that dedicate it reveal what it means to be
church—living stones, a spiritual house, a holy priesthood."

—Bernadette Gasslein, Editor, *Worship*

"Fr. Paul Turner has produced a wonderful commentary including
rich historical references for a ritual that few people ever get to
experience in person. Vicariously we can experience it through
his writing."

—Michael S. Driscoll, Professor Emeritus of Theology,
University of Notre Dame

New Church, New Altar

*A Commentary on the Order of
Dedication of a Church and an Altar*

Paul Turner

✞

LITURGICAL PRESS
Collegeville, Minnesota

www.litpress.org

The English translation of Psalm Responses from *Lectionary for Mass* © 1969, 1981, 1997, International Commission on English in the Liturgy Corporation (ICEL); the English translation of Non-Biblical Readings from *The Liturgy of the Hours* © 1973, 1974, 1975, ICEL; excerpts from the English translation of *Ceremonial of Bishops* © 1989, ICEL; excerpts from the English translation of *The Roman Missal* © 2010, ICEL; excerpts from the English translation of *The Order of the Dedication of a Church and an Altar* © 2014, ICEL. All rights reserved.

Excerpts from documents of the Second Vatican Council are from *Vatican Council II: Constitutions, Decrees, Declarations; The Basic Sixteen Documents*, edited by Austin Flannery, OP, © 1996. Used with permission of Liturgical Press, Collegeville, Minnesota.

1	2	3	4	5	6	7	8	9

Library of Congress Cataloging-in-Publication Data

Names: Turner, Paul, 1953- author.
Title: New church, new altar : a commentary on the order of dedication of a church and an altar / Paul Turner.
Description: Collegeville, Minnesota : Liturgical Press, [2021] | Includes bibliographical references. | Summary: "An aid for parish leadership and students of liturgy in preparing the celebration of the dedication of a church with greater understanding of the history, spirituality, and practical aspects of the liturgy" — Provided by publisher.
Identifiers: LCCN 2021014576 (print) | LCCN 2021014577 (ebook) | ISBN 9780814666593 (paperback) | ISBN 9780814666609 (epub) | ISBN 9780814666609 (mobi) | ISBN 9780814666609 (pdf)
Subjects: LCSH: Catholic Church. Dedication of a church and an altar. | Catholic Church—Liturgy. | Church dedication—Liturgy. | Altars.
Classification: LCC BX2302.C373 T87 2021 (print) | LCC BX2302.C373 (ebook) | DDC 265/.92—dc23
LC record available at https://lccn.loc.gov/2021014576
LC ebook record available at https://lccn.loc.gov/2021014577

IN MEMORIAM EPISCOPI SVI
RAYMONDI BOLANDI
QVI OPVS SVVM
TAM PASTORALEM QVAM THEOLOGICVM
ADHORTATVS EST
ATQVE FORMAM ÆDIS
ECCLESIÆ SANCTI IOHANNIS FRANCISCI REGIS
PROBATVS EST
HVNC VOLVMEN DEDICAT AVCTOR

Contents

Abbreviations

CB	*Ceremonial of Bishops*
Durand	*Le pontifical romain au Moyen Âge, Tome III, Le pontifical de Guillaume Durand*
GIRM	The General Instruction of the Roman Missal
ODCA	*Order of Dedication of a Church and an Altar*
PR 1595–1596	*Pontificale Romanum: Editio princeps*
PR 1961	*Pontificale Romanum*
PRG	*Le Pontifical Romano-Germanique du Dixième Siècle*

Introduction

"Church," happily, means both building and people. That one word in English captures the interplay between the physical building and the persons who believe in what it represents.

At certain momentous times, a church dedicates a church. The celebration brings to fruition the hopes, plans, meetings, fundraising, wisdom, excitement, disappointments, and dreams of a community. Parishioners behold a new space where they will gather, a space that affirms their identity and shapes their praise of God.

Central to a new church is a new altar. Its dedication seals the relationship between the building and the worship it houses. Sometimes an older church receives a new altar. Its solemn dedication honors its sacred function.

Canon law declares that a church is a sacred building set apart for divine worship. The faithful have the right to enter it for that purpose.[1] The *Ceremonial of Bishops* notes that the purpose of a church building is to gather the Christian community "to hear the word of God, to pray together, to celebrate the sacraments, and to participate in the eucharist."[2]

---

1. *Code of Canon Law* (Washington, DC: Canon Law Society of America, 1983), canon 1214.

2. *Ceremonial of Bishops* (CB) (Collegeville, MN: Liturgical Press, 1989), p. 864.

Only a bishop can authorize the construction of a Catholic church.[3] Only a bishop may dedicate the church or its altar, although he may delegate another bishop or priest to do so.[4] The dedication should take place as soon as possible because the space is not sacred until this ceremony happens, and until then, Mass is to be celebrated there only in case of necessity.[5]

The day for the dedication must be carefully chosen. The date will become an annual solemnity to be observed on the parish calendar for the entire life of the building. For this reason, the law excludes certain days: Christmas, Epiphany, Ash Wednesday, Holy Week, the Paschal Triduum, Ascension, Pentecost, and All Souls' Day.[6] However, it therefore permits the dedication liturgy to replace a Sunday in Advent, Lent, Easter, and Ordinary Time. Prudence excludes feasts that the parish may wish to celebrate but which the Mass on the anniversary of dedication would replace; for example, the commemoration of the parish's titular saint or of a day already attracting strong devotion, such as Our Lady of Guadalupe (December 12).

The title bestowed on the church at its dedication is permanent. Only one saint may be given the title, except for saints listed together in the calendar.[7] This means that if a parish is ever combined with another parish, the original dedicated name of the church cannot change, though the name of the parish community may.

The liturgy for the events is found in the *Order of Dedication of a Church and an Altar*. This ritual has been thoroughly revised since the Second Vatican Council (1962–1965), and it successfully incorporates the ecclesiology of the council into

---

3. Canon 1215 §1.

4. Canon 1207 and CB 867, 923.

5. Canon 1217 §1 and §2, 932 §1; and CB 922.

6. *Order of Dedication of a Church and an Altar* (ODCA) (Washington, DC: United States Conference of Catholic Bishops, 2018), II:7.

7. Canon 1218; ODCA II:4; and CB 865.

its ritual acts. Although published independently, this order of service is considered part of a larger work called the Roman Pontifical, the collection of ceremonies over which a bishop presides. The *Order of Confirmation* is another example of a book that actually forms part of the Roman Pontifical, though it is published as an independent ritual.

In 1961, just before the opening of the council, the Vatican had authorized an initial revision of these ceremonies as part of an updated Roman Pontifical, the fruit of the liturgical renewal already underway. While the council was still in session, a new committee met in 1965 to begin revising the Pontifical again, but other projects took priority, such as the liturgical books pertaining to the Mass, as well as orders of service for baptisms and weddings, celebrations important to Catholic families.[8] Furthermore, because the Order of Dedication had just been modified, work on that project was tabled until yet another new committee shouldered the task in 1970.[9] After drafting the new format and sending it out to various dioceses for comments, the committee finalized its work within a few years, and the Vatican published its typical edition in Latin in 1977.[10] A provisional English translation appeared in 1978[11] and again in 1989.[12] The Vatican published new rules for

8. Jean Evenou, "Le nouveau rituel de la dédicace," *La Maison-Dieu* 134 (1978): 85–105. For this reference, p. 87.

9. Annibale Bugnini names the relator as Pierre Jounel of France and the members as Ignacio Calabuig, OSM, from Spain, Canon André Rose from Belgium, and Domenico Sartore from Italy. *The Reform of the Liturgy 1948–1975*, trans. Matthew J. O'Connell (Collegeville, MN: Liturgical Press, 1990), pp. 792–97.

10. *Ordo Dedicationis Ecclesiæ et Altaris* (Vatican City: Typis Polyglottis Vaticanis, 1977).

11. *Dedication of a Church and an Altar* (Toronto: International Committee on English in the Liturgy, 1978).

12. *Dedication of a Church and an Altar*, Provisional Text, rev. 1989 (Washington, DC: United States Conference of Catholic Bishops, 1989).

vernacular translations in 2001, which initiated a revision of
all the liturgical books in English. Because the Roman Missal
took priority once again, absorbing considerable effort until its
publication in 2011, work on the various parts of the pontifical
was deferred. The revised *Order of Confirmation*, for example,
was not ready until 2016. The revised English translation of
The Order of the Dedication of a Church and an Altar (ODCA)
carries a publication date of 2018.

The International Commission on English in the Liturgy
(ICEL) is charged with preparing the translations of the liturgical books from the typical editions in Latin into the
vernacular. The commission published a summary and brief
commentary on the ODCA in late 1977. It noted several highlights, especially the decision to change the dedication from a
ceremony taking place just before the celebration of the first
Mass in the building, to a place inside that very Mass:

> [T]he ancient centrality of the eucharist in this act of dedi-
> cation has been restored to its proper place. As the summit
> towards which the worship of the liturgical assembly tends,
> the celebration of the eucharist is the most suitable means
> of dedicating the altar and church where this worship will
> now take place. . . .
>
> The rite and its introduction also present a compelling
> and renewed sense of the pre-eminence of the worshiping
> community as the primary liturgical symbol. The building
> is significant as the gathering place of the faithful. It is this
> which makes it a holy place.[13]

The new typical edition provides a liturgy that moved from a
focus on the exorcism and blessing of sacred space to the dedication of a church—both the building and the people. Ignazio

13. "Rite for the Dedication of a Church: A Commentary," *ICEL Newsletter*
4/4 (October–December 1977), pp. 2–3.

Calabuig, OSM, who served on the revision committee, wrote about the task:

> The liturgical point of the rite had been smothered by a profusion of signs. Simplification of this sort necessarily entailed the pruning away of parts valid in themselves, but which in their accumulation—like an excess of fine furniture in an overcrowded room—made for a good deal of clutter.[14]

Still, many will find the ceremonies quite complex, especially because most people may experience them only once in a lifetime. Furthermore, the ODCA covers more circumstances than the dedication of a new church and altar, which is sufficiently intricate by itself. Consequently, the first task upon picking up the book is to discern which of its rituals apply to the project at hand.

Chapter I contains The Order of Laying a Foundation Stone or the Commencement of Work on the Building of a Church. This pertains to the initial stage of construction of a new church, usually of a parish church. The bishop appropriately presides even for this event, but he may entrust his role to another bishop or a priest (ODCA I:3).

Chapter II presents The Order of the Dedication of a Church. This is the most significant chapter in the book because it concerns both the dedication of the church and its altar, carried out simultaneously in the same liturgy within the celebration of the Eucharist.

Chapter III has The Order of the Dedication of a Church in Which Sacred Celebrations Are Already Regularly Taking Place. This covers a situation that is not recommended but

---

14. Ignazio M. Calabuig, OSM, *The Dedication of a Church and an Altar: A Theological Commentary* (Washington, DC: United States Catholic Conference, 1980), p. 5.

can happen: The building has been serving as a church long before any bishop has dedicated it. Now, the time has come.

Chapter IV contains The Order of the Dedication of an Altar. This may be used, for example, when an existing church acquires a new altar as part of a renovation, requiring the bishop to dedicate it.

Chapter V is The Order of Blessing a Church. Different from Chapter II, this concerns the blessing of a chapel, oratory, or other building for sacred purposes, together with its altar. It does not include all the complex rituals of the dedication of a parish church, for example.

Chapter VI presents The Order of Blessing an Altar. Different from Chapter IV, this concerns the blessing but not the dedication of an altar. For example, a parish may set up an altar in a room suitable for daily Mass, or a priest on mission may need to bring his own altar. Such a furnishing receives this blessing.

Chapter VII contains The Order of Blessing a Chalice and a Paten. Any priest may conduct this ceremony (ODCA VII:3), but it has a long tradition associated with the Roman Pontifical because it used to require a bishop to anoint the new vessels with chrism. In a nod to the tradition, the revised order of service retains it in the final chapter.

Obviously, not all of these chapters can apply to the construction project of a single given community. Some of them are mutually exclusive. But one or more of these chapters will be needed. As the United States bishops have remarked, "Just as the initiation of a person into the Christian community occurs in stages, so the construction of a church building unfolds over a period of time."[15] Once the appropriate rituals have been identified, liturgical preparations may begin.

---

15. *Built of Living Stones: Art, Architecture, and Worship, Guidelines of the National Conference of Catholic Bishops* (Washington, DC: United States Catholic Conference, 2000), 118.

On the anniversary of the dedication of a church, the local parish celebrates the day as a solemnity. The Mass and the Liturgy of the Hours come from the Common of the Dedication of a Church. At Mass, special readings are selected among the many options in the lectionary; the antiphons, presidential prayers, and preface come from the appropriate place in the Missal. The conclusion of this book makes remarks on observing both the anniversary of dedication and the titular saint of the church.

At a dedication, the local priest and those who assist him prepare readings, music, and other aids to foster the participation of the people (ODCA II:19 and CB 872). They are also to instruct the faithful "on the spiritual, ecclesial, and missionary importance and value of the celebration" (ODCA II:20). The same pastoral care fittingly applies to the celebrations presented in the other chapters of the ODCA and to the parish's annual local solemnities. To that end, a companion booklet accompanies this book, suitable for distribution among the people who will celebrate these events.[16]

From breaking ground on the first day of construction to remembering the founders of the parish on its annual anniversary, this book hopes to assist especially those who lead the church at their church.

16. Paul Turner, *Our Church, Our Altar: A People's Guide to the Dedication of a Church and Its Anniversary* (Collegeville, MN: Liturgical Press, 2021).

The Order of Laying a Foundation Stone or the Commencement of Work on the Building of a Church

After the bishop has approved the construction of a new church and is satisfied that the necessary material and spiritual resources are available, the community gathers to celebrate the ritual described in the first chapter of the ODCA. If the project is of smaller scale—the building of a chapel, for example—or if the community already has been using a building not yet dedicated, the ritual in this chapter is omitted.

The physical work of construction commences with the spiritual work of prayer. The community gathers outdoors, preferably with the bishop who will eventually dedicate the new church. A wooden cross marks the location where the altar will be. The ceremony takes place without Mass, which will not be celebrated here until the bishop returns to dedicate the completed building. Still, this ritual carries a profound meaning: The gathering of the people on location proclaims that "the structure to be built of stones will be a visible sign of the living Church, God's building" (ODCA I:1).

The ceremony therefore calls to mind 1 Corinthians 3:9, where St. Paul calls his readers God's building, as well as the

Second Vatican Council's Constitution on the Church, *Lumen Gentium*, which lists Paul's image among several that apply to a proper understanding of the church (6).

A wooden cross marking the site of the altar has been part of this ritual since the thirteenth century. The Pontifical of William Durandus, a work that the eponymous bishop of Mende wrote for his own usage, became treasured throughout the church and influenced the development of the Roman Pontifical after the Council of Trent. Durandus wrote at the beginning of his description of this same ritual, "At dawn therefore a wooden cross should be set in the place where the altar will be."[1]

In 1965, when the Vatican's committee began its soon-to-be-deferred efforts to revise this ritual from the pontifical of 1961, the members still managed to create a vision that endures:

> For the Order of Blessing and Laying a Foundation Stone for the Building of a Church.
>
> When the stone has been blessed, and, if it will have seemed desirable, when the document of the blessing of the foundation stone and of the beginning of the church has been read, it should be in complete conformity to the spirit of the Constitution on the Sacred Liturgy, so that something from Sacred Scripture is read, as for example those matters recounted concerning the building of the Temple of Solomon in Deuteronomy (*sic*), or another passage. At the end, though, or while the stone is being laid, some popular song may be sung. When the rite is completely finished, it is ap-

---

1. *Le pontifical romain au Moyen Âge, Tome III, Le pontifical de Guillaume Durand* (Durand), Studi e Testi 88, ed. Michel Andrieu (Vatican City: Biblioteca Apostolica Vaticana, 1940), II:I, 2, p. 451. English translations from such works are by the author.

propriate that a hymn or canticle of thanksgiving be sung by all the people.[2]

This results in an order of blessing in four main parts: The Approach to the Place Where the Church Is to Be Built, The Reading of the Word of God, The Blessing of the Site of the New Church, and The Blessing and Laying of the Foundation Stone. All this ends with The Concluding Rites.

Part One: The Approach to the Place Where the Church Is to Be Built

The ceremony begins either with a procession to the site or a gathering on the site. The First Form calls for the community to gather in another location where the bishop greets them and offers a prayer (ODCA I:10–13). His prayer praises God, "who established Holy Church, built upon the foundation of the Apostles with Christ Jesus himself as chief cornerstone." The bishop thus directly connects this event to the description of the church in Paul's letter to the Ephesians 2:20. The prayer concludes with a desire that the people may "come at last to the heavenly city." Here the bishop alludes to the image of the new Jerusalem in Hebrews 12:22 and Revelation 21:02.

The same prayer also looks back in history to the construction of the temple of Solomon, the greatest and most beloved building project in the Old Testament. The bishop prays that the gathered people may "revere," "love," and "follow" God. According to 2 Chronicles 7:14, God expected these same sentiments from those who worshiped in Solomon's newly built temple, as revealed to the king in a dream. The bishop also

2. Coetus a Studiis XXI de Libris II et III Pontificalis, Schemata n. 67, De Pontificali, 4, March 25, 1965, I:3, p. 2.

prays that the people may "grow into the temple of [God's] glory," another allusion to Solomon's building, which was filled with the glory of the Lord (2 Chr 7:1). The bishop thus places this project within the arc of buildings dedicated to God from the earliest moments of biblical history.

The entire English translation passed through several stages of work with ICEL, beginning in 2009.[3] The bishop's prayer went through a few minor changes; for example, the Latin word for "revere" is *timeat*, which the translators had first rendered as "fear." Although "fear of the Lord" is a common concept in biblical piety, the word "revere" seemed better to capture its contemporary meaning.

Then the deacon invites all to move to the building site. That procession may include the singing of Psalm 84 with the refrain, "My soul is longing for the courts of the Lord" (ODCA I:14). This psalm had been part of the ceremony in the Roman Pontifical of 1595–1596,[4] which remained in force until 1961, but the schola sang it, not the people, and not in procession but at the time when the bishop sprinkled the ground and the cross with water he had just blessed. For hundreds of years, this liturgy included no processional music or gathering hymn because the ministers conducted it largely without the presence of the people. Today, the gathered people of God form one of the primary symbols of the rite.

In the Second Form of The Approach to the Place Where the Church Is to Be Built, the people begin the ceremony by

3. The author serves as a facilitator for the commission and shares some of his personal recollections in this book.

4. *Pontificale Romanum: Editio princeps (1595–1596)* (PR 1595–1596), ed. Manlio Sodi, SDB, and Achille Maria Triacca, SDB (Vatican City: Libreria Editrice Vaticana, 1997), pp. 290–92. See also the commentary by the papal master of ceremonies Joachim Nabuco, *Pontificalis Romani expositio: Juridico-practica*, Domus II: De Rebus (New York: Benziger Brothers, 1945).

singing a suitable chant. The rubrics suggest a trinitarian text: "May eternal peace from the eternal God be with those gathered here. May abiding peace, the Word of the Father, be peace for the people of God. May the faithful Consoler, bring peace to all nations" (ODCA I:15). Then the bishop greets the people and offers the prayer that precedes the procession in the first option.

An early draft of the English translation for this prayer made the trinitarian structure clearer by adding the words "the Spirit," followed by a comma, before the words "the faithful Consoler." However, the word "Consoler," the sole title in the original Latin, sufficiently conveys the meaning. That explains the wayward comma that remains in the ritual text after the word "Consoler." The editors overlooked removing it when they eliminated the words "the Spirit" and the correlative comma.

Both forms of this first part contain new material that the postconciliar reform added to the ODCA in order to strengthen the meaning of the rites. The bishop's prayer concerns the people, not just the building, that they may "grow into the temple" of God's glory. The ceremony repositions one of the psalms originally sung on pilgrimages to the Jerusalem temple as processional music to the site. The people's trinitarian acclamation places the work into the hands of God, the bestower of peace. Even the mention of the Consoler in the acclamation reflects the council's commitment to more frequent mentions of the role of the Holy Spirit in the church's collection of prayers. Whereas Durandus began the rite with sprinkling holy water to purify the site, the ceremony now begins with a purposeful assembling of the church.

Part Two: The Reading of the Word of God

Catholics expect a Liturgy of the Word at public gatherings for worship, but biblical readings had not been part of this ceremony before the reforms of the Second Vatican Council. The ceremony did include, however, a generous selection of psalms.

One or more readings may be proclaimed. Although people may anticipate one reading, a psalm, and a gospel, as they experience at a daily Mass, the Reading of the Word of God may be simplified to one passage (ODCA I:18). This makes accommodation for the practical reality that this ceremony is taking place outdoors, possibly in inclement weather and without adequate seating for the participating assembly.

Of the four options for the first reading (I:19), the first recounts the beginning of the construction of the temple of Solomon (1 Kgs 5:16-32 or 2-18). Many communities may avoid selecting this passage because of its length, but the compelling account provides a vast historical setting for the work now underway. This is surely the passage that the original committee envisioned in 1965, one that it mistakenly assigned to Deuteronomy. In the second option, Isaiah prophesies about a cornerstone that God is laying in Zion (Isa 28:16-17). This prophecy, to be fulfilled in Christ, uncovers the purpose of the future building. From Acts of the Apostles, Peter proclaims that Jesus fulfills a similar prophesy in the psalms about the rejected stone that becomes the cornerstone (4:8-12). In the First Letter to the Corinthians, Paul shows that the rock from which Israel drank in the desert was none other than Christ (10:1-6). In all four of these options, the community hears a connection between the laying of the first stone of their building with biblical passages foreshadowing or declaring Christ as the cornerstone of redemption and faith.

For the responsorial, there are five possibilities (ODCA I:20). Psalm 24:1-2, 3-4ab, 5-6 is another pilgrimage song, this time paired with a phrase from the Second Book of Chronicles (7:16a), where God proclaims his consecration of Solomon's new temple. Psalms 42:3, 5bcd, and 43:3-4 are paired as another prayer of pilgrimage. Psalm 100:2, 3, 5 serves the same purpose, though it receives an antiphon based on Ezekiel 37:27, in which God proclaims that his dwelling place will be among the people. Psalm 87:1-3, 4-5, 6-7 proclaims the holiness of the city of Zion, where God dwells in the temple. The verses selected from Psalm 118 are the ones that inspired Peter's preaching in the reading from Acts, and they are paired with another line based on Paul's First Letter to the Corinthians (3:11), where he proclaims that Jesus Christ is the only foundation that can be laid.

There is no gospel acclamation. This probably reflects the absence of a procession to an ambo. It also reminds those preparing the liturgy that they may choose a reading, psalm, and gospel as typically happens at a daily Mass, but they need not. Only one or two readings may be proclaimed, with or without a psalm. This is not Mass, and Part Two is called "The Reading of the Word of God," not "The Liturgy of the Word."

The gospel may come from four options (ODCA I:21). During the Sermon on the Mount (Matt 7:21-29) and the parallel sermon on the plain (Luke 6:46-49), Jesus praises the house built on the solid rock of his teaching. In Matthew 16:13-18, Jesus promises to build his church on the rock of Peter's faith, a passage referenced in the dialogues that formed part of this opening ceremony in the sixteenth-century pontifical.[5] From Mark's gospel (12:1-12), Jesus compares himself to the cornerstone imagery in Psalm 118. Once again, the options focus more on the rock, the beginning of the project and the foundational role of Christ, than the building.

The homily that follows explains the readings and the meaning of the rite: "Christ is the cornerstone of the Church, and the structure that is going to be built by the living Church of

5. PR 1595–1596, p. 292.

the faithful will be at once the house of God and the house of the People of God" (ODCA I:22). Thus, the second part of the ceremony shows additional influence of the ecclesiology of the Second Vatican Council, the importance of the Word of God, and the significance of both the building and the people it represents.

Someone at the parish may prepare a document recording the blessing of the stone and the beginning of the construction (ODCA I:23). The rubrics say nothing further about its contents, but it would helpfully preserve at least the date of the ceremony and the names of at least some of the participants. At the conclusion of the homily, someone may read this, and the bishop and representatives of those who will work on the building may sign it. It is thus prepared to be embedded in the building with the cornerstone. This custom resembles the traditional placing of a time capsule inside even secular structures.

The person chosen to read the document would fittingly have some connection to the events that led up to this day; it could be the pastor, someone from the building committee, or even an elderly or very young parishioner. The bishop and the workers may sign the document ahead of time or at this moment. Although this part of the ceremony is optional and new to the history of the rite, it helps sanctify the work about to be undertaken.

Part Three: The Blessing of the Site of the New Church

The third part takes place in two halves: The bishop immediately prays a blessing for the people, and then he sprinkles the site with blessed water (ODCA II:24–25). Once again, the liturgy pairs the people with the building. If the bishop processes around the site, all may sing Psalm 48 or another appropriate song. The recommended refrain is based on a passage from Isaiah 54:12, which promises the restoration of the exiled people and the rebuilding of their beautiful temple after its capture and destruction: "All your walls will be of precious stones and the towers of Jerusalem built with gems."

This psalm occupies the place where the preconciliar liturgy had Psalm 84. Moving Psalm 84 to become an option at the beginning of this celebration gave it greater integrity as a processional hymn. By adding Psalm 48 as an option to this moment when the bishop may walk around the site of the future building, sprinkling water on the areas where the walls will rise, the liturgy draws a fitting parallel between his actions and a verse such as 13: "Walk through Zion, walk all around her."

Part Four: The Blessing and Laying of the Foundation Stone

Some new church buildings do not employ a foundation stone; in those circumstances, this part is omitted. Where there is a stone, the bishop blesses it with a prayer that Christ, the beginning and end of all things, "may be the origin, progress, and fulfillment of this work." The bishop may then sprinkle the stone with blessed water, and he may incense it. He may set the stone in place silently or with a declaration of faith in Jesus Christ and a prayer that his name will be "invoked and praised" in the building to be raised (ODCA II:26–28).

The bishop's prayer deftly combines allusions to several biblical passages: Daniel 2:45, 1; Corinthians 3:11; and Revelation 1:8 and 22:13. The Latin original of this prayer simply refers to "the Prophet" and "the Apostle," but the names of Daniel and Paul were added to the English translation for clarity. Christians interpret Daniel's prophecy about a virginal, uncut stone freed from a mountain as a reference to the miraculous incarnation of Jesus in the womb of a virgin. Paul calls Christ the firm foundation, and Revelation calls him the alpha and omega of all things. The allusion to the passage in Revelation where Jesus calls himself the Alpha and the Omega beautifully draws the first and last chapters of the last book of the Bible into the opening ceremony at the construction of a new church. Durandus made this prayer richer and more precise in purpose than its predecessors in the thirteenth-century pontifical of the Roman Curia,[6] and the version in today's ritual is based on his work.[7]

Similarly, the bishop's optional declaration of faith and prayer is based on Durandus.[8] He opens with a seemingly insignificant phrase, "In the faith of Jesus Christ," but this probably alludes to James 2:1, where the epistle encourages readers to adhere to the faith in the Lord Jesus Christ. The bishop concludes with the acclamation, "To him be glory and power for all the ages of eternity," which captures an expression from Revelation 1:6.

As a stonemason fixes the rock in place, optionally together with the signed document that has been read, all may sing an antiphon such as the one inspired by Matthew 7:24, "The house of the Lord is founded firmly, on solid rock." In Easter Time, the antiphon concludes with an alleluia (I:29).

In the late 1950s, the Vatican established a pontifical commission to prepare what became the revised Roman Pontifical of 1961. Notes from those meetings show that when the ceremony for laying the foundation stone came under discussion,

---

6. *Le pontifical romain au Moyen Âge, Tome II, Le pontifical de la Curie Romaine au XIIIe siècle* (Vatican City: Biblioteca Apostolica Vaticana, 1940), XXI and XXII, pp. 420–21.

7. Durand II:II, 6, p. 452.

8. Durand II:II, 23, p. 453.

the members saw the importance of keeping it. They believed that in this ritual, the envisioned building was already taking possession of the ground.[9] Having the bishop preside showed the spiritual importance of this first phase of construction.

The Concluding Rites

Several steps bring the ceremony to a fitting close. The bishop introduces the universal prayer, and a deacon or another minister lists the petitions, to which all may respond, "Bless and preserve your Church, O Lord." All recite the Lord's Prayer to conclude the intercessions, and the bishop offers a concluding prayer. He then blesses the people, and the deacon dismisses them (ODCA I:30–31).

The bishop's introduction to the universal prayer again draws the parallel between the building and the people.[10] As the physical church is to rise, the bishop prays that God will make the people "into the living temple of his glory."

The petitions as usual are to be delivered "in these or similar words." One may read them directly from the ritual, adjust them for the local celebration, or replace them with new ones. Nonetheless, these make rich reliance on passages from the Bible. One petition asks that God will always set the workers for the project "on the solid rock of his Church," recalling Matthew 7:24. By praying that those who cannot erect churches may "build themselves into a living temple," the community hears an echo of Ephesians 2:21-22. The petition for

9. Nicola Giampietro, *The Development of the Liturgical Reform as Seen by Cardinal Ferdinando Antonelli from 1948 to 1970* (Fort Collins, CO: Roman Catholic Books, 2009), p. 304, nn. 1058 and 1059. See also p. 309, n. 1121.

10. Luke Chengalikavil, "La Dedicazione della chiesa e dell'altare," *Anamnesis 7: I Sacramentali e le benedizioni* (Genoa: Marietti, 1989), p. 85.

the worthiness of those present calls them "living stones hewn and dressed by God's hand," combining references to 1 Peter 2:5 and Daniel 2:45.

In the concluding prayer, the bishop focuses again on the people. He glorifies God for entrusting the construction of churches to those who were baptized into a holy temple, and he asks that "they may grow into the temple of your glory, until, shaped by your grace, they are assembled by your hand in the heavenly city." This calls to mind the coming of the glory of the Lord into the temple of Solomon (2 Chr 7:1) and again in the prophetic vision of Ezekiel (43:4-5). The word "shaped" translates the unusual Latin word *expoliti*, which can mean "polished." God, then, is the ultimate builder who polishes and assembles the people into a sacred building where his glory will dwell.

This opening ceremony, built on ancient precedents and enriched with new material, sets the tone for the dedication of the church and its altar at the conclusion of the time of construction.

CHAPTER II

The Order of the Dedication of a Church

This chapter contains the main ceremony of the ODCA. It envisions the completed construction of a new church building with a new altar and the arrival of the bishop to preside over the dedication. Other chapters of the book are preliminary (I), derivative (III, IV, V, and VI), or ancillary (VII). The community that witnesses this celebration of dedication will possess the memory of a lifetime, and future generations will praise God for the founders' achievements.

The dedication of the church's new altar may include the positioning of relics of a saint. If so, the ceremonies may begin the night before the dedication. People may gather to pray the Office of Readings from the Common of the Dedication of a Church or from the proper office of the church's titular saint (ODCA II:10). As a prologue to the dedication, the community gathers for a vigil to pray in the presence of the relics of the saint.

This custom can be traced to a letter of St. Ambrose (+397), bishop of Milan, who received the newly discovered relics of the local martyr saints Gervase and Protase. The people experienced such joy in the presence of the relics that they asked

Ambrose to delay their deposition in the altar for a day of prayer.[1] Such an observance today would heighten the anticipation of the dedication of the entire building the following day.

When a new church is ready for use, its dedication will be a day of true celebration for the community. Calabuig notes its significance:

> The dedication of a church, consequently, is the occasion for joy over the completion of a work which required effort, sacrifice, and unremitting toil. The dedication of a church also provides the propitious moment for the local Church to see itself as the true "Temple of God," to renew its obligation to "build itself" as the Church, and to increase its membership, its "living stones."[2]

James E. Healy recommends careful preparation to involve many members of the community in the liturgy.

> Spread the roles around, especially these most visible ones at the liturgy. You have worked hard through all these processes and consultations to make this a church built by the parish and not by a select few. Don't let it slip here at the last minute with a committee-dominated dedication ceremony. Involve as many people and segments of the parish as possible. Broad representation in the liturgy is not only good politics; it is good theology because it makes visible the variety of the people of God.[3]

---

1. Ambrose of Milan, Letter XXII:25, 23, *Nicene and Post-Nicene Fathers*, ed. Philip Schaff and Henry Wace, ser. 2, vol. 10 (New York: The Christian Literature Company, 1896), pp. 438–40.

2. Calabuig, "Commentary," p. 6.

3. James E. Healy, *Building a New Church: A Process Manual for Pastors and Lay Leaders* (Collegeville, MN: Liturgical Press, 2009), p. 128.

In his commentary on this ceremony, Thomas G. Simons describes the importance of the day of dedication.

> The dedication of a church points to a unique and characteristic moment in the life of a local Church. A Church may exist without literal and physical walls. Christ is the reason for its existence, and the Holy Spirit is the wellspring of its life. Yet, since the pilgrim Church on earth cannot exist outside the limits of space and time, it usually erects buildings that are the visible counterparts of the invisible "building of God" (1 Corinthians 3:9), the place where the faithful meet in their worship or in holy assembly.[4]

The bishop fittingly presides for the dedication, but he may entrust the duty to another bishop or even a priest (ODCA II:6). Priests who aid him in the dedication ceremony or who have responsibility for the people associated with this church appropriately concelebrate the Mass (ODCA II:9 and CB 869). They all vest in white due to the festive nature of the gathering (ODCA II:23 and CB 870).

The celebration of Mass is "inseparably linked" to the dedication (ODCA II:8), but this was not the case in the past. Sometimes the Mass alone dedicated the altar, and sometimes the dedication unfolded in a ceremony completely separate from the Mass.

The earliest reference to a church dedication comes from the father of church history, Eusebius of Caesarea (+339). At that time, the first celebration of the Eucharist in the new space sufficed for its dedication. The ceremonies for the new cathedral at Tyre, for example, resounded with the singing of psalms and

---

4. Thomas G. Simons, *Holy People, Holy Place: The Rites for the Dedication of a Church and an Altar* (Chicago: Liturgy Training Publications, 2020), p. 28.

prayers and with the "divine and mystical ministrations";[5] that is, the celebration of the Eucharist. John Chrysostom wrote, "This altar is an object of wonder; by nature it is stone, but it is made holy after it receives the Body of Christ."[6] An early decretal attributed to either Pope Evaristus (+ c. 107) or Pope Hyginus (+142), but surely dates long after them, says, "All basilicas should be consecrated with Mass."[7]

Later testimony shows that the opposite happened: Churches were dedicated completely apart from Mass. An eighth-century Byzantine ritual spread the ceremony over two days: "on the first, the bishop consecrates the altar in the presence only of the clergy; on the second, in the presence of the entire people, he inaugurates the new building for worship and dedicates it to the Lord."[8]

In the West, the earliest descriptions of a dedication ceremony in the developing Roman Rite come from Gallic and Roman Sources. The ninth-century Gallic Ordo XLI describes the entire ceremony of the dedication of a church in a few brief pages, then adds, "After all these things, [the schola] may then

5. Eusebius, *The History of the Church*, trans. G. A. Williamson (Harmondsworth: Penguin Books, 1965), X:3, 3, p. 383.

6. ODCA II:17 and IV:23. For another translation, see *Nicene and Post-Nicene Fathers 12, Chrysostom: Homilies on the Second Epistle of St. Paul the Apostle to the Corinthians*, Homily XX:3, p. 374.

7. Pierre Jounel, "The Dedication of Churches," *The Church at Prayer: An Introduction to the Liturgy*, ed. Aimé Georges Martimort (Collegeville, MN: Liturgical Press, 1992), I:217, citing the Decretals of Gratian III, *De consecr.*, Dist. 1, c. 3 (ed. A. Friedberg, col. 1294).

8. Ignazio M. Calabuig, OSM, "The Rite of the Dedication of a Church," *Handbook for Liturgical Studies, Volume V, Liturgical Time and Space*, ed. Anscar J. Chupungco, OSB, A Pueblo Book (Collegeville, MN: Liturgical Press, 2000), p. 347, citing the *Codex Barberini* and S. Salaville, *Cérémonial de la consécration d'une église selon le rite byzantin avec introduction et notes explicatives* (Vatican City: Vatican Polyglot Press, 1937).

begin the entrance antiphon. And the bishop processes from the sacristy with his clergy, as is the custom, and they celebrate Mass as it is contained in the Sacramentary."[9] Ordo XLII, also from the ninth century, is of Roman origin and similarly describes the dedication in a few brief pages. It concludes with this note: "When this has been completed, the schola sings the entrance antiphon and, after the *Kyrie eleison*, the *Gloria in excelsis Deo* is sung, and the Mass is carried out in its order."[10] Even in the thirteenth century, the dedication ceremony stood distinct from the Mass: "When everything has been finished, the bishop goes back to the sacristy and, while the church is decorated and lighted with torches, he dresses for Mass, as the cantor begins the introit."[11]

The first edition of the full Roman Pontifical of the sixteenth century gave the bishop another option when he completed the dedication of the church and altar: "After [the response] has been said, the bishop goes up to the sacristy or the sanctuary, where, his cope having been removed, he prepares himself to celebrate Mass, if he so desires, or he arranges it to be celebrated solemnly by some priest on the aforementioned consecrated altar."[12] The Mass was so distinct from the dedication that the bishop may not even have presided for it. This remained the case into the twentieth century.

In 1977, the revised order placed the dedication of the church and the altar completely within the Mass. The celebration of the Eucharist is "inseparably bound up" with the dedication (CB 869). Even when conferences of bishops seek to adapt this

---

9. *Les Ordines romani du haut Moyen Âge, IV Les Textes*, ed. Michel Andrieu (Leuven: Spicilegium Sacrum Lovaniense, 1985), Ordo XLI:30, p. 347.

10. Ordo XLII:19, p. 402.

11. Durand II:II, 100, p. 477.

12. PR 1595–1596, p. 441.

liturgy, "the celebration of the Mass with its proper Preface and the Prayer of Dedication must never be omitted" (ODCA II:18a). As Calabuig notes, "a perfect seam unites the celebration of the memorial of the Lord and the *Rite of Dedication of a Church*."[13]

Part One: The Introductory Rites

The entrance into the church takes place in one of three ways: with a procession outdoors that starts at some walking distance, with a gathering just outside the door of the church, or completely inside the new building (ODCA II:11 and 28, and CB 879). In preparation for the entrance, it would be fitting for the electrical lights of the church to be switched off. These may be illumined when the candles are lit for the first time later in the ceremony (ODCA II:71).

First Form: The Procession

In the First Form, the people gather in a nearby church or other suitable place. If relics are to be placed solemnly under the altar, they are honorably present with the people. The door to the new church is closed (ODCA II:29 and CB 880).

Calabuig comments, "the rite reflects the truth of the situation: as light comes from light (the symbolism of the lighting of the candles in the Easter Vigil), as faith generates faith (the rite of baptism), so does one community emerge from another."[14] The people from one house of worship give birth to another.

The very mention of the people expresses the ecclesiology of Vatican II. Chapter II of *Lumen Gentium*, the council's Constitution on the Church, emphasized the significance of the

---

13. Calabuig, "Commentary," p. 32.
14. Calabuig, p. 7.

entire people of God. In the previous pontifical, the people were mentioned, but not until after the bishop and the clergy.[15] Now the clergy are listed after a paragraph noting the presence of the people (ODCA II:30).

The importance of the presence of the people is not new. In the fifth century, St. Augustine (+430) preached these words: "We are gathered together to celebrate the dedication of a house of prayer. This is our house of prayer, but we too are a house of God."[16] In the sixth century, St. Caesarius of Arles (+542) preached, "My fellow Christians, today is the birthday of this church, an occasion for celebration and rejoicing. We, however, ought to be the true and living temple of God."[17]

Today the bishop begins the liturgy by greeting the people as usual or with a special formula: "May grace and peace be with you all in the holy Church of God" (ODCA II:30). Calabuig notes that the intent of this greeting "is to emphasize from the very outset the ecclesial sense of the rite."[18] It is richer than "The grace and peace of God," the simpler greeting suggested in CB 881. ICEL had originally reversed the ODCA's phrases in order to give a better cue to the people: "In the holy Church of God may grace and peace be with you all." The greeting seems to have evolved from one found in the thirteenth century Pontifical of Durandus, where, once inside the church, the bishop said, "Peace to this house and to all who dwell in it,"[19] in turn

15. PR 1961, p. 304.

16. Augustine, Sermon 336, 1.6, *Liturgy of the Hours*, Common of the Dedication of a Church, Office of Readings, Second Reading, Alternative.

17. Caesarius of Arles, Sermon 229, 1–3, *Liturgy of the Hours*, November 9, Dedication of Saint John Lateran, Office of Readings, Second Reading. Evenou cites both these patristic quotes, "Le nouveau rituel," p. 105.

18. Calabuig, "Commentary," p. 7.

19. Durand II:II, 39, p. 462.

based on the greeting that Jesus told his disciples to deliver upon entering homes on mission (Luke 10:5).

The sign of the cross that begins a typical Mass is missing. It is not clear if that was an oversight or a deliberate deletion because this unusual liturgy begins outside sacred space, and the cross will lead all in procession. In the thirteenth century, Durandus had the bishop use the lower end of his pastoral staff to trace the sign of the cross on the lintel of the church's door just before entering the building, but this had an exorcistic function. The bishop said, "Behold the sign of the cross; let all evil spirits flee."[20] The third edition of the Roman Missal added a sign of the cross to the beginning of the liturgies of Palm Sunday and the Easter Vigil, where no mention had been made in previous editions. The rubrics that open the funeral Mass remain silent about the initial sign of the cross. Here, one could argue either that the bishop's greeting of the people suffices because the 2016 translation of the ODCA did not correct the omission or that the bishop begins with the sign of the cross in imitation of the clarified rubrics from other places in the Missal.

The bishop tells the people about the purpose of their gathering and invites them to participate, so that they "may grow into a spiritual temple." The full address was enriched after the first draft by adding to the phrase "reborn from the one font of Baptism"[21] the expression "nourished at the same table." Calabuig notes that "the admonition follows the greeting, as if the latter had coherently turned into exhortation and instruction."[22] A similar structure had opened the postconciliar

20. Durand II:II, 37, p. 462.
21. See Coetus a Studiis 21 bis, *Ordo Dedicationis Ecclesiae*, Schemata n. 370, De Pontificali, n. 24, 8 October 1970, p. 1, n. 4, where this is missing.
22. Calabuig, "Commentary," p. 8.

Mass for Palm Sunday of the Lord's passion in the first edition of the Missal, where the admonition superseded the greeting.[23] The third edition added the greeting to Palm Sunday.

The cross leads the procession toward the church. No incense is carried because it will be introduced later in the rite. Similarly, no candles join the procession except to accompany relics if these are present. Assisting ministers follow the cross, then come those who carry and attend the relics, extra deacons, concelebrants, the bishop accompanied by two deacons, and the rest of the faithful (ODCA II:31). Calabuig says of this,

> The order of the procession reflects the ordered composition of the local church. . . . The Church on its journey follows the cross of Christ. Moreover, when the procession also involves the transferral of relics of martyrs or saints it is well to stress that, in so doing, the Church follows in the steps of its members who have given lofty witness to the following of Christ.[24]

All may sing the recommended Psalm 122 with its refrain, "Let us go rejoicing to the house of the Lord" (ODCA II:32 and CB 882). This draws a connection between past pilgrims to the Jerusalem temple and the community processing to the new church and, ultimately, to the heavenly Jerusalem.[25] From at least the thirteenth century, the schola sang this psalm a little later inside the new church as the bishop completed sprinkling blessed water around the interior.[26] The retention of

23. Paul Turner, *Glory in the Cross: Holy Week in the Third Edition of* The Roman Missal, A Pueblo Book (Collegeville, MN: Liturgical Press, 2011), p. 5.

24. Calabuig, "Commentary," p. 9.

25. Calabuig, p. 9.

26. *Pontifical romain au Moyen Âge, Tome II, Pontifical de la Curie Romaine*, XXIII:41, p. 431 and PR 1595–1596, p. 333.

such psalms was one of the earliest recommendations for the revision of these rites after the Second Vatican Council.[27] The revisers moved this one forward to a more expressive place in the procession toward the new church.

The procession stops outside the threshold of the new building. Representatives of the faithful, donors, architects, and builders hand the church over to the bishop. They may give him legal documents, plans, or the keys. Someone may explain the art and design to the bishop. The bishop then calls upon the priest responsible for the community to open the door of the people's new church, handing him the key (ODCA II:33 and CB 883). Calabuig notes, "In the history of the rites for the dedication of a church, this encounter constitutes a new ritual sequence that seeks to express, in liturgical terms, the value of an old, deeply human, and Christian reality: the labor of people for the building of the church."[28]

Of this gathering at the threshold in preparation for entering the building, the USCCB notes, "As the diocesan bishop celebrates the Rite of Dedication and receives the church from his people, the connection between the diocesan Church and the parish community is particularly evident."[29] Besides the physical documents and keys that the bishop receives, the explanation of the art and architecture is also important because, as Calabuig notes, "a church also has a soul."[30]

The group preparing this liturgy after the Second Vatican Council added the conversation at the threshold in its first draft, giving this explanation: "The new church is presented to

27. Schemata 370 III:B2.
28. Calabuig, "Commentary," p. 9.
29. *Built of Living Stones*, 120.
30. Calabuig, "Commentary," p. 10.

the bishop by a delegation of those who produced the work of building it; in this way human labor is praised and extolled."[31]

When the door is unlocked, the bishop invites the people inside. He may use his own words, or he may quote the fourth verse of Psalm 100: "Enter the gates of the Lord with thanksgiving, his courts with songs of praise." The people may sing Psalm 24 or another chant. The recommended refrain is, "Grow higher, ancient doors. Let him enter, the king of glory" (ODCA II:34 and CB 884). The people who first sang that verse improbably yet confidently commanded the inert gates of the Jerusalem temple to expand, making room for the immense glory of the Lord to enter. A similar sentiment applies to this moment.

The freshness and simplification of this ceremony will escape many of those who participate. In the history of the rite, the ceremonies outside the church used to include a blessing of water and an exorcism of the property. For example, the practice of sprinkling water of exorcism, as recorded in the twelfth century pontifical,[32] continued through other pontificals, all the way to the 1961 edition.[33] The sprinkling has been completely removed at this part of the ceremony to clarify the initial symbols and to make room for a sprinkling inside the building that not only purifies but renews the baptismal covenant of those who are the church.

As early as the ninth century, twelve candles were lighted inside the church before the ceremony began.[34] When the

---

31. Schemata 370, p. IV, n. 3a.

32. *Le pontifical romain au Moyen Âge Tome I, Le pontifical romain du XIIe siècle*, ed. Michel Andrieu (Vatican City: Biblioteca Apostolica Vaticana, 1938) XVII:13–9, pp. 177–78.

33. *Pontificale Romanum* (PR 1961), ed. Anthony Ward, SM, and Cuthbert Johnson, OSB (Rome: CLV Edizioni Liturgiche, 1999), pp. 130–31.

34. Ordo XLI:1, p. 339.

procession reached the door, the bishop struck the lintel three times with his pastoral staff, saying the antiphon, "O gates, lift up your heads," and others sang all of Psalm 24. When the door opened, those entering said, "Peace to this house," recalling Luke 10:5.[35]

The ceremony grew more elaborate in the ensuing centuries. Subsequent pontificals had the bishop engage in a dialogue with a deacon previously positioned inside. In the twelfth century, for example, the bishop rapped on the church door with his pastoral staff and called out verse 7 from Psalm 24: "O gates, lift high your heads; grow higher, ancient doors. Let him enter, the king of glory." The deacon within responded with verse 8, "Who is this king of glory? The Lord, the mighty, the valiant; the Lord, the valiant in war." They conducted this dialogue three times, punctuating a procession that the bishop led around the church exterior, accompanied by prayers. Finally, the deacon opened the door to the singing of the antiphon, "Zacchaeus, hurry and come down; for I must stay at your house today. So he hurried down and was happy to welcome him. Alleluia. Today salvation has come to this house" (Luke 19:5-6, 9).[36]

The singing of Psalm 24 near the beginning of this ceremony can be traced to the sixth century rededication of Hagia Sophia.[37] Calabuig notes,

> The opening of the door in the rite is of ancient origin. It goes back, for its inspiration, to the rite of the dedication of the basilica of Santa Sophia in Constantinople which took place on December 24, 562. . . . All former theatrical elements, however, have been removed from the rite. The natural move-

35. Ordo XLI:2, p. 340.
36. *Pontifical romain au Moyen Âge, Tome I, XII*, XVII:10-17, pp. 178–80.
37. Andrieu, "Le rituel de *L'Ordo XLI*: Son origine Gallicane, date," p. 316.

ment of entrance, it is recognized, is by itself a more than adequate expression of a liturgical act.[38]

In the preparation of the 1961 pontifical, its committee wanted to retain the beginning of Psalm 24 with its command to open the gates, but sung by all and only once.[39] In the completed pontifical, the people's acclamation followed a dialogue between the bishop and the deacon reciting the opening verses of the same psalm.[40]

As the postconciliar revision was underway, some discussion centered on the verse that the people would sing with Psalm 24 as they first entered the building. In the first draft, the bishop declared the verse from Psalm 100 that remains in the rite, as well as the opening of Psalm 24 passed from him to the people: "Lift up, O gates, your heads, and grow higher, ancient doors."[41] Even this verse underwent a small adjustment so that it now gives the reason for opening the gates: "Let him enter, the King of glory." This historic psalm remains recommended in the ceremony, but with a new purpose. Formerly sung outside the threshold, it now becomes the true entrance hymn. It replaces for the first time the Litany of the Saints that had marked the entrance of the bishop into the new building from the ninth century[42] to the 1961 pontifical.[43] The litany remains in the ceremony, but it is deferred to a more expressive ritual moment.

Psalm 24 draws many allusions: the arrival of the pilgrims at the temple in Jerusalem, the entry of the ark of the covenant

38. Calabuig, "Commentary," p. 10.
39. Giampietro, *Development of the Liturgical Reform*, p. 305, n. 1067.
40. PR 1961, p. 131.
41. Schemata n. 370, p. 2, n. 8.
42. Ordo XLI:3, p. 340.
43. PR 1961, pp. 131–33.

into the tent of David, the incarnation of Jesus, his triumphal entry into Jerusalem, his entry into heaven at his ascension, and his coronation as Christ and Lord of all.[44]

Therefore, when the bishop today asks the priest in charge of the building to open the door and invites the people inside, he is performing a naturally expressive act that is new to the postconciliar ceremony. For many centuries, a deacon previously stationed inside the church opened the building to the bishop. Now the door opens from the outside: the priest responsible unlocks it for the first time, and the people enter in song. Calabuig notes, "[the priest] must open the hearts of the faithful to knowledge of the mysteries of the Kingdom, just as with his life, in imitation of the Good Shepherd, he is to be the door of the sheepfold."[45]

Once inside the building, the bishop goes to the presider's chair without reverencing the altar with a bow or a kiss, and all take their places. If relics have been carried, these are set in a place of honor between two candles (ODCA II:35 and CB 885). The bishop is the first to take possession of the chair in the new church. It functions as his cathedra for this occasion.[46]

Once again, the postconciliar ceremony has simplified all its predecessors. Beginning in the ninth century, during the Litany of the Saints, when the ministers arrived in front of the altar, they prostrated themselves for its remainder, then stood and knelt for additional prayers inside the new building.[47] These postures and petitions have been removed, creating a leaner entrance into the new church, along with more focus on the prayers and postures that remain.

44. Calabuig, "Commentary," p. 11.
45. Calabuig, p. 11.
46. Calabuig, p. 12.
47. Ordo XLI:3, p. 340.

Also removed was a signature ceremony that had endured ever since its appearance in the ninth century through 1961: "Then the bishop begins from the eastern left corner, writing the Latin alphabet on the pavement with his pastoral staff, up to the western right corner; similarly beginning again from the eastern right corner, writing the Greek alphabet, up to the western left corner."[48] By the twelfth century, a minister sprinkled ashes on the pavement so that the inscribed letters would better stand out, and the bishop reversed the alphabets, starting with the Greek in the eastern left corner.[49] Even the 1961 pontifical retained the ceremony, which it called a "possession" of the church, as if the bishop were claiming the ground for Christ, the Word made flesh.

The writing of the alphabets may have originated in medieval Ireland. Andrieu cites favorably the research of Herbert Thurston, who notes the custom of Roman surveyors dividing the floor of a church into four equal rectangles and the Irish custom of writing an alphabet onto church pavements. Even the unusual Latin word for the pastoral staff that the bishop used to knock on the lintel and write on the pavement suggests an Irish origin for these ceremonies. "Thurston concludes that the alphabet thus written on a diagonal crossing is nothing but the development of the symbol of the alpha and omega from the Book of Revelation (1:8), in addition to the chrism, both images of Christ."[50]

Why was writing alphabets removed from the ritual? The postconciliar revisers in general do not explain all their reasons, but perhaps in this case they thought that the opening ceremonies already boasted symbols aplenty, that inscribing

48. Ordo XLI:5, pp. 340–41.

49. *Pontifical romain au Moyen Âge, Tome I, XII*, 18–20.

50. Andrieu, "Le rituel nouveau," pp. 319–20.

of letters across the church's diagonals was logistically complex, that the use of the vernacular rendered the writing of foreign alphabets obsolete, and that some abbreviations would enhance the people's overall experience of the liturgy. When the bishop and the people of God enter the building, they are already claiming it for Christ.

Second Form: The Solemn Entrance

If logistics prohibit an outdoor procession, the people gather just outside the new church. If the relics of a saint are to be embedded beneath the new altar, these are set temporarily where people gather. Ideally, the bishop and other ministers arrive with the people from outside the closed doors of the church; if necessary, however, they may walk from inside the church to the place where the people have gathered. The bishop leads the opening dialogue and gives the address as in the First Form. At its conclusion, people may sing an antiphon, but probably not the entirety of Psalm 122, because no procession is yet moving anywhere. The dialogue with those who helped the building project continues as in the First Form, but if the door is already open, the bishop does not entrust the key to the priest responsible for the building. The entrance happens as in the First Form (ODCA II:36–42 and CB 886–889).

Third Form: The Simple Entrance

If even the second form cannot be used, then the entire liturgy begins inside the building where the people have already gathered. The vested ministers process behind the cross from the sacristy, through the church, into the sanctuary. If relics are present, these may be carried in this procession or suitably displayed between two candles (ODCA II:43–44).

In the preconciliar liturgy, just before the bishop inscribed the alphabets, the schola used to sing, "How awesome is this place! This is none other than the house of God, and this is the gate of heaven" (Gen 28:17).[51] Jacob exclaimed those words after his dream of angels ascending and descending the ladder to heaven.

Now a similar antiphon has been retained as a suggestion only in this third form of the entrance: "God is in his holy place, God who unites those who dwell in his house; he himself gives might and strength to his people." It is recommended together with Psalm 122 (ODCA II:45). This antiphon had been the introit in the preconciliar Missal for the Eleventh Sunday after Pentecost, and the group preparing the revised rite of dedication suggested placing it here in its 1970 draft.[52] The antiphon still appears in the Missal on the Seventeenth Sunday in Ordinary Time, along with the citation Psalm 68:6-7, 36.

The antiphon from the first two forms is permitted as a secondary option: "Let us go rejoicing in the house of the Lord." Because the people are already inside the house of the Lord, the first antiphon better acknowledges their presence inside God's holy place.

The bishop goes to the chair without kissing the altar, then greets the people as he does at the beginning of the first two forms. His address, however, is omitted. The dialogue with the representatives of the project takes place inside the church, and the bishop does not hand a key to the responsible priest because people are already inside the building. All references to Psalm 24 are omitted because the community has already gathered inside, eliminating the need to sing the psalm that calls upon the gates of the holy place to open (ODCA II:46–47 and CB 890–891).

---

51. PR 1961, p. 138.
52. Schemata 370, n. 18, footnote.

The reasons for choosing the Third Form may relate to physical space: The church may have been constructed in a location where the people have no room outside to gather. Or there could be societal challenges, as Calabuig notes: "In many places throughout the world, laws forbid the congregation of the faithful outside the church for the purpose of ritual; elsewhere, a convocation of this sort for a variety of reasons would be inopportune."[53]

In none of the forms do the rubrics give clear instructions pertaining to the crossbearer. However, since the cross may be brought forward to the altar later in the ceremony (ODCA II:69), it is appropriately set to the side once the procession enters the church, even if it will serve the parish as the altar cross in the future.

The Blessing and Sprinkling of Water

The bishop blesses water to be sprinkled on the people as a sign of their repentance and a remembrance of their baptism. This recalls its purpose in holy water stoups at church entrances (CB 110) and as an optional replacement for the penitential act of Sunday Mass (Roman Missal Appendix II, Rite for the Blessing and Sprinkling of Water, 1). At the dedication of a church, blessed water is sprinkled not just on the people, but also on the inner walls and on the altar (ODCA II:48).

The bishop invites the people to join him in prayer not just over the water but over themselves, "that, docile to the Spirit whom we have received, we may remain faithful in his Church." The bishop's prayer praises God who cleanses people from their sins and makes them heirs to an eternal reward. It also asks that the action "may be a sign of the cleansing waters of salvation" (II:48 and CB 892).

---

53. Calabuig, "Commentary," p. 7.

The bishop then sprinkles the people, the walls and the altar as all sing an antiphon such as "I saw water flowing from the Temple" (Ezek 47:01, 09), which is also the first option in the Missal for the sprinkling of water on Sundays. An alternative from Ezekiel 36:22-26 is proposed for dedications taking place during Lent: "When I prove my holiness among you, I will gather you from all the foreign lands, and I will pour clean water upon you and cleanse you from all your impurities, and I will give you a new spirit" (II:49 and CB 893).

In the next chapter of the ritual book, the order of dedicating a church already in use omits the sprinkling of the walls because of its purificatory nature (ODCA III:2c). The bishop still sprinkles the people, but their prior use of the building has already purified its walls. This helps clarify the purpose of sprinkling the walls in Chapter II: It prepares the building for worship.

The prayer of blessing water alludes to many biblical passages: Romans 6:3-7 (dying with Christ in the waters of baptism), 1 Corinthians 6:19 (humans as temples of the Spirit), and both Hebrews 12:22 and Revelation 21:2 (the heavenly Jerusalem). It also employs a variety of aquatic images: "dew of charity," "sacred waters" (or "waves" in Latin), "sprinkled" water, "cleansing waters," and "washed in Christ." Calabuig notes that the five different Latin words behind these images show "the diverse ways in which the one and multiform divine mercy expresses itself."[54]

Usually, a blessing and sprinkling of water at the beginning of Mass takes place only on a Sunday. Because of the special nature of this sprinkling, its conclusion was newly composed for the ODCA and kept unique to this celebration. The bishop says, "May God, the Father of mercies, dwell in this house of

54. Calabuig, p. 15.

prayer and, by the grace of the Holy Spirit, cleanse us who are the temple where he dwells" (ODCA II:50 and CB 894). The bishop refers to 1 Corinthians 3:16-17, where Paul calls his readers the temple where God's Spirit dwells. Concerning this new formula, Calabuig notes, "Placed at the conclusion of a rite with penitential aspects, it has the typical structure of a deprecatory absolution. It intertwines two expressions that run through the rite—house of prayer (*domus orationis*) and dwelling place (*templum habitationis*) the two realities that denote the divine presence."[55]

Catholics are somewhat accustomed to a sprinkling rite at the beginning of a Mass, but this one introduces a new sequence of events in the history of the opening ceremonies for the dedication of a church and an altar. In the preconciliar ceremonies, two sprinklings took place, one before the procession that crossed the threshold of the church and another after the dedication of the altar. In neither of them did the bishop sprinkle water on the people, whose presence was rarely noted in rubrics of the past.

In the ninth-century Ordo XLI, after the bishop wrote the alphabets on the floor of the church, he approached the altar. There he blessed a mixture of salt, water, and ashes, and he exorcized the salt, using prayers from other sources, such as the eighth-century Gelasian Sacramentary.[56] He added wine to the mixture and used his finger to sprinkle it on the four corners of the altar. Dipping a branch of hyssop into the mixture, he walked around the altar seven times, sprinkling the water upon it and also upon the walls of the church. The bishop dispatched other ministers to sprinkle the outside walls of the building. He sprinkled the pavement of the church. Coming to the altar,

55. Calabuig, p. 15.
56. Ordo XLI:7-8, p. 341, with commentary on pp. 320 and 335.

he poured what was left of the water onto the base of the altar and dried it with cloth.[57]

In Ordo XLII, also from the ninth century, in order for the bishop to position relics properly at the beginning of the service, he blessed water, added chrism to it, and used some of the liquid to make a paste that he used to seal the relics into the altar. He sprinkled the altar with more blessed water.[58] The complete sprinkling of the altar and the walls of the church followed the anointing and covering of the altar in cloths.[59]

As Calabuig notes, it is not known whether the sprinkling, "when first used, was applied indiscriminately or only in those instances, quite frequent after the peace of Constantine, in which the new church arose on a former pagan site, or was actually the transformation of a former pagan temple."[60] Pope Gregory the Great prescribed this rite to St. Augustine of Canterbury when the pope sent the bishop to England:[61]

> Temples of idols ought to be destroyed at least among the same people, and let those idols that are within them be destroyed. Let blessed water be made and sprinkled on the same temples, let altars be constructed, and relics placed there, because if the same temples had been well built, it is necessary that they should be changed from the worship of demons into devotion of the true God.[62]

---

57. Ordo XLI:10–17, pp. 342–44.

58. Ordo XLII:4–6, pp. 398–99.

59. Ordo XLII:17, p. 402.

60. Calabuig, "Commentary," p. 12.

61. Jounel, *Church at Prayer*, I:218, citing St. Gregory the Great, *Regist.* XI, *Ep. 56.*, ed. Ewald-Hartmann, MGH, *Epist.* 2 (Berlin, 1891), 331.

62. Andrieu, Ordo XLII: "La dédicace des églises à Rome et la déposition des reliques," p. 373.

Calabuig says that the letter of Pope Vigilius to Profuturus of Braga in 538 shows that "the washings are not necessary in the dedication of a restored church, thereby letting it be understood that they were customary in other dedications,"[63] such as the dedication of a converted pagan temple.

By the sixteenth century, the rite of sprinkling had become even more elaborate. After writing the alphabets, the bishop blessed salt, ashes, water, and wine, and mixed them while reciting a series of prayers and exorcisms. The resulting liquid came to be known as "Gregorian water." He began the consecration of the altars of the church by sprinkling this water upon them, circling the altar seven times. He sprinkled the walls, walking around the church three times. He sprinkled the pavement, east, west, north, and south. All of this took place amid many psalms, prayers, and genuflections.[64] The ceremony of sprinkling served as an immediate prelude to the consecration of the altar.

This began to change in 1961. The entire ceremony started outside the church with the use of Gregorian water, which for the first time could have been prepared in advance. The bishop led the gathered assembly around the church exterior three times, sprinkling the walls.[65] Inside the church, after the Litany of the Saints, the bishop sprinkled the interior walls with a branch of hyssop dipped in Gregorian water, all to a simplified sequence of psalms and prayers. Approaching the altar, he signed it by dipping his right thumb in the water and tracing crosses on the altar's center and four corners.[66] This

---

63. Calabuig, "Rite," p. 344, citing *Epistola ad Profuturum Bracarensem* 4, *Patrologia Latina* 69:18.

64. PR 1595–1596, p. 321–39.

65. PR 1961, p. 130.

66. PR 1961, pp. 134–36.

preceded the writing of the alphabets, separating the sprinkling of the altar from its consecration with chrism. The bishop wore violet vestments from the beginning of the ceremony through the sprinkling and the writing of the alphabets, changing to white for the placement of the relics before the consecration of the church and altar.[67] Thus even his vesture showed the penitential purpose of sprinkling water.

The former ceremony focused on a purification of the building for sacred use, an elaborate exorcism to keep demonic forces from influencing a Christian gathering. Calabuig notes how this has changed: The sprinkling "is retained in order to stimulate the assembly's spirit of conversion, to recall the rite of baptism and the first steps of the Christian's journey."[68] In the revision, the prayers were completely adjusted to indicate this new purpose, and the water is sprinkled on the people, partly as a reminder of their baptism, not just on the building to purify its walls.

The first draft of the postconciliar rite carried this commentary with these stresses: *"All symbols of the previous Ordo have been preserved*, some things having been changed. *The blessing of water* (baptismal or not baptismal) and *the sprinkling of the people* exist in place of the rites of the purification of the building; the substance (*res*) of the rite is the church established by the people, not the church built from stones."[69] The draft presented alternate versions of the blessing, depending on whether or not the water would also be used for baptisms. The second draft explained that the water not used for baptism was blessed only for the purpose of sprinkling the people.[70] The

67. PR 1961, pp. 130 and 141.
68. Calabuig, "Commentary," p. 13.
69. Schemata 370, III A2a, p. III.
70. Schemata 375, 25, p. 6.

ritual eventually dismissed the distinction between baptismal
and non-baptismal water.

In the first draft, however, the bishop positioned himself at
the font to bless any water to be used for future baptisms. If
people could not see the font, minsters were to bring a bowl
of water into view, thus facilitating the people's participation.
That blessing was to be taken from the Order of Baptism of
Children. Whether or not the bishop prepared water for future
baptisms, he sprinkled everyone with the water he blessed,
walking through the church.[71]

The alternate version for water not to be reused for baptism
is the one that remains in place today. The bishop's introduction, addressed to the people, originally made use only of baptismal imagery,[72] but the final version includes the notion of
repentance as well. This retained a stronger connection to the
preconciliar rite.

For the blessing of water, the first draft simply borrowed
one from the Missal,[73] but a new one was composed to enrich
the imagery and purpose of the blessing. Instead of exorciz-
ing things, this water blesses the people rescued from sin by
baptism. As Calabuig notes, this action "gives humanity the
central place but does not forget the things of this world."[74]
The addition of the antiphons from Ezekiel helped modify
a purification rite to one with a more baptismal character.[75]

The sprinkling ranks among several symbols in the order
of dedication that resemble those of Christian initiation, as
though the building were undergoing initiation as well: the

71. Schemata 370, 23–25.
72. Schemata 370, 26.
73. Schemata 370, 26.
74. Calabuig, "Commentary," p. 14.
75. Calabuig, p. 15.

gathering at the door, the sprinkling with blessed water, the Litany of Saints with the addition of the name of the patron, the anointing with chrism, the covering with a white cloth, the lighting of candles, and the celebration of the Eucharist. Joseph Jungmann noted the similarities in 1949: "church and altar are 'baptized' and 'confirmed' almost like human beings; they are sprinkled on all sides with holy water and are anointed with holy oil; only after that is the first Eucharist celebrated."[76] Calabuig argues, however, that "this parallelism was not deliberately sought by the authors of the ancient *ordines*; nevertheless, the parallelism did become both a key for interpreting the entire rite and a guide to its structure."[77] He cites the allegorical readings of Ivo of Chartres (+ 1115) and the 1961 revision, which used the initiation sacraments as a guiding idea.

The Hymn and the Collect

After the sprinkling, all sing the Gloria and the bishop offers the collect of the Mass (ODCA II:51–52 and CB 894). This draws to its close Part One of the liturgy, The Introductory Rites. It also gives the gathered community of the faithful some familiar markers: They sing a Gloria on festive occasions; they pray along silently with the collect, sit afterwards, and open their ears to the Liturgy of the Word.

With the collect, the bishop asks God to "pour out your grace upon this place" and to "extend the gift of your help to all who call upon you, that the power of your word and of the Sacraments may strengthen here the hearts of all the faithful." Again, one sees the connection between the people and the building.

---

76. Joseph Jungmann, *The Mass of the Roman Rite: Its Origins and Development*, trans. Francis A. Brunner (Notre Dame: Christian Classics, 2012), I:254.

77. Calabuig, "Rite," p. 344.

This collect replaces a different one from the early drafts of the revised rite: "O God, who were pleased to call the Church your people, grant that the people gathered in your name may revere you, love you, follow you, and may be led by you to attain your promises in heaven."[78] This is a version of the same collect that now opens The Order of Laying a Foundation Stone or the Commencement of Work on the Building of a Church (ODCA I:13 and 17), complete with its reference to the way that people were to respond to God in the Jerusalem temple, as revealed in a dream to Solomon (2 Chr 7:14). A version of this prayer remains in the Missal as an alternate collect for the Common of the Dedication of a Church, On the Anniversary of the Dedication, II: Outside the Church That Was Dedicated. According to ICEL's researchers, the original came from the Gelasian Gellone Sacramentary of the eighth century.

The same postconciliar drafts had positioned the prayer that now serves as the collect in a different place: to conclude the blessing of the altar before the beginning of the eucharistic prayer. Eventually the revisers determined that no prayer was necessary at that point. Rather than completely eliminate this one, the committee moved it forward to serve as the collect.

The earliest version of the collect in force comes from the eighth-century Gelasian Sacramentary as the first prayer for the dedication of a new basilica: "O God, who sanctify places dedicated under your name, pour out your grace upon this house of prayer, that the help of your mercy may be felt by all who call upon you here."[79] As was the custom, the bishop offered that prayer during the ceremony that took place apart from Mass.

---

78. Schemata 370, 29, and Schemata 375, n. 28, p. 7.

79. *Liber Sacramentorum Romanæ Æclesiæ Ordinis Anni Circuli* (Gelasian Sacramentary), ed. Leo Cunibert Mohlberg (Rome: Casa Editrice Herder, 1981), 689.

During the Mass that followed the dedication, the Gelasian Sacramentary records a second version of the same prayer as the secret or prayer over the offerings.[80] Its words form a prayer that is almost identical to the one that now serves as the collect. The original prayer, however, did not mention the Word of God. The contemporary version edited in a reference to "the power of your word and of the Sacraments." This new phrase indicates both the Liturgy of the Word and the Liturgy of the Eucharist that will take place in this house of prayer, and the two parts of the Mass that now for the first time in history frame the Order of Dedication.

Part Two: The Liturgy of the Word

All take their seats, but two readers and a psalmist approach the bishop, one of the readers carrying the lectionary. The bishop stands, shows the lectionary to the people, and proclaims, "May the word of God resound always in this building to open for you the mystery of Christ and to bring about your salvation in the Church" (ODCA II:53 and CB 895). The verb "shows," *ostendit*, is the same Latin word used during the eucharistic prayer of every Mass when the celebrant "shows" the newly consecrated host and chalice to the people (Order of Mass 89, for example). The same verb describes the way the priest "shows" the host to each communicant while saying, "The Body of Christ" (Order of Mass 134). It suggests the reverence that the people collectively hold for the Word of God. As they do individually at communion, the people together answer, "Amen." The bishop hands the lectionary to the reader.

---

80. Gelasian Sacramentary, 711.

The postconciliar revisers proposed this new element in their first draft.[81] The same draft envisioned that a deacon or another minister would carry the lectionary to the bishop, who, without showing it to the people, handed it to the first reader and made his declaration, while the reader alone answered, "Amen."[82]

The second draft still had the deacon or another minister carrying the lectionary but introduced the presence of the two readers and the psalmist. The bishop handed the lectionary to one of them, made his declaration, and all three answered, "Amen."[83] The final version kept the deacon away from this ceremony, which pertains to the first readings, and incorporated the participation of the people with their "Amen."

The showing of the lectionary bears some similarity to the presentation of the lectionary to new catechumens in their rite of acceptance. The celebrant explains the purpose of the Liturgy of the Word to the catechumens, and a minister may incense the lectionary before the first reading.[84] Here, the showing of the lectionary to the people, its procession to the ambo, and the formal opening of the book for the first time fittingly serve as a prelude for the first reading.

The first reading at this liturgy is always Nehemiah 8:1-4a, 5-6, and 8-10 (ODCA II:54a and CB 896). In that passage, Ezra brought out the book of the law of Moses into the view of the people in Jerusalem, stood on a newly constructed wooden platform, solemnly opened the book, and read it before the entire assembly with clarity, so that the people could understand. The parallels to the present ritual are unmistakable.

---

81. Schemata 370, III, 3b, p. IV.
82. Schemata 370, n. 30.
83. Schemata 375, n. 29, p. 7.
84. *Rite of Christian Initiation of Adults*, 61.

Even if the dedication takes place during Easter Time, when the first reading is generally to come from the New Testament, the Old Testament passage of Nehemiah must be proclaimed.[85] One reason the dedication liturgy may not take place on certain solemnities of the church year, such as Pentecost, is to avoid a conflict of first readings.

The first reading effectively dedicates the ambo. The bishop never sprinkles it with blessed water, nor incenses it, nor offers any prayer of blessing over it. The second draft of the postconciliar rite made this explicit in a rubric that has been removed: "By this reading [from Nehemiah], where the solemn proclamation of the law of God to the people is described, the ambo, from which the Word of God will be announced to the faithful, is in a certain way dedicated."[86]

Calabuig notes, "As a liturgical reality however, the ritual has broader implications: it underscores the value of the proclamation of the word, which calls the community into being and is itself an essential moment in our faith."[87] Furthermore, the choice of the reading from Nehemiah "becomes a symbol of the rite in which the community gathered around the Gospel of Christ celebrates . . . the birth of a church."[88]

The idea for the reading from Nehemiah was proposed in the first draft of this liturgy, which also assigned responsorial psalm 119:105-109 with the refrain, "Your word, O Lord, is a light for my steps."[89] This eventually changed to Psalm 19B:8-9, 10, 15, with a refrain from John 6:63c, "Your words, Lord, are Spirit and life." Peter had spoken that faithful declaration

85. ODCA II:12.
86. Schemata 375, n. 30, p. 8.
87. Calabuig, "Commentary," pp. 16–17.
88. Calabuig, p. 18.
89. Schemata 370, III B1 (p. IV).

to Jesus when some disciples deserted him after hearing the discourse on the Bread of Life. The Book of Blessings includes these passages from Nehemiah and Psalm 19 as options for the blessing of a new lectern (1184). Easy to overlook, the ODCA offers no other options for the responsorial psalm. It considers Psalm 19 and the refrain from John's gospel the only possible response of the people to the reading from Nehemiah. This responsorial serves as the people's fitting reply to the first proclamation of the Word, their pledge to find in God's Word both Spirit and life.

By contrast, the possible selections for the second reading, gospel acclamation, and gospel are numerous. The ODCA refers those preparing the liturgy to 816 in the Lectionary for Mass, which in turn refers them to passages in 704 (and two passages from 702 in Easter Time) for the second reading, and to 705 and 706 for the gospel acclamation and gospel respectively.

In 1 Corinthians 3:9c-11, 16-17, Paul calls his readers the temple of God in whom the Spirit dwells. This passage is much referenced throughout the liturgies of the ODCA.

In Ephesians 2:19-22, Paul calls his readers members of the household of God built upon the apostles and prophets with Christ as the capstone. The architectural imagery also makes this passage a favorite reference point in the various ceremonies of dedication.

The letter to the Hebrews 12:18-19, 22-24 describes one's mystical participation in a heavenly liturgy in the city of the living God. Worshipers in the present new building hope to participate in the eternal Jerusalem at the end of their days.

The First Letter of Peter 2:4-9 invites readers to come as living stones built into a spiritual house, a holy priesthood offering sacrifices. The liturgies of dedication often pair this image with that of Christ as cornerstone. The altar represents the foundation stone of Christ, while the walls of the church represent the living stones of the Christian people.

In Easter Time, a passage from the Bible's last book may be chosen. Revelation 21:1-5a envisions the holy city, Jerusalem, coming down out of the heavens, God dwelling with the human race. Revelation 21:9-14 describes that city in more detail, including its twelve gates, three each facing east, north, south, and west. This latter passage stands behind the custom of anointing the walls of the new church.

The lectionary offers several options for the Alleluia verse and verse before the gospel.

Second Chronicles 7:16 reports the words of the Lord as he appeared to Solomon in a dream upon the completion of the construction of the temple in Jerusalem. The Lord has chosen and consecrated the temple as his own house.

Isaiah 66:1 is the Lord's humbling rhetorical question: How could anyone build a house for the one who made the heavens and the earth?

In Ezekiel 37:27, the Lord speaks to a people weary of exile that his dwelling will again be with them.

In Matthew 7:8, Jesus promises that those who knock on the door of the Lord's house will have their prayers answered.

In Matthew 16:18, Jesus promises to build his church on the solid rock of Peter's faith.

Similarly, those preparing the liturgy may choose from a selection of gospel passages.

Matthew 16:13-19 reports the conversation between Jesus and Peter, where Peter proclaims his confident faith and Jesus pledges to build his church upon that rock. This newly constructed church stands on the solid faith of generations past.

In Luke 19:1-10, Jesus commands Zacchaeus to descend from the tree so that he may stay at Zacchaeus's house. Jesus' desire to enter the dwelling of a believer offers a particularly fitting lens for those inviting the glory of God into their new church home to interpret this popular account.

In John 2:13-22, Jesus drives out the merchants and money changers from the temple, declaring the sacred space his Father's house. This dramatic image previews the emotional attachment that the followers of Christ apply to a church building.

In John 4:19-24, Jesus converses with the woman at the well, explaining that, no matter where people worship, they must worship God in Spirit and truth. The dedication of the new building, as elaborate as it is, does not replace the believer's personal duty to worship sincerely.

No matter which gospel is chosen, the procession does not include candles or incense (ODCA II:54b). Both symbols will be unveiled later in the ceremonies of dedication.

The first draft of the postconciliar rite had introduced yet another symbol at this point: "As a sign of veneration toward the Word of God, it is praiseworthy that, after the reading of the gospel, the book of readings be set onto an appropriate stand before the people."[90] This suggestion was ultimately removed, perhaps because the Missal does not explicitly call for the book of readings to remain on view at any Mass after the proclamation of the Word. It does say that the book is set at the credence table or "another suitable and dignified place" (GIRM 275). That does not exclude some kind of enthronement, though the first suggestion of using the credence table clearly has a less visible location in mind. Nonetheless, the bishops of the United States have acknowledged the custom of setting the book of the gospels on a more permanent display in the sanctuary, for example, "the front of the ambo or another kind of pedestal" (*Built of Living Stones*, 62, n. 84).

90. Schemata 370, n. 32.

The bishop delivers the homily, "in which he explains the biblical readings and the meaning of the rite" (ODCA II:55). CB 897 says further that he explains the readings and "the rite by which the church building is dedicated to God and the growth of the Church is fostered." This was surely inspired by the comment in the first draft, which had him explain the rite by which the growth of "the local and the universal Church is fostered."[91]

Perhaps the earliest example of a homily at such an occasion is the one recorded by Eusebius. The author was probably also the preacher who delivered this quite lengthy talk at the dedication of the cathedral in Tyre (c. 315).[92]

The community recites the Creed, but the universal prayer is omitted because of the Litany of the Saints, soon to be sung (ODCA II:56 and CB 898). The first draft envisioned this differently: "The Creed is not said, even if it is prescribed by the rubrics of the liturgical day."[93] In the final version, the Creed is said even when *not* prescribed by the liturgical day. The people of the church profess their common faith inside the new church. This brings the second part of the liturgy to a close.

Part Three: The Prayer of Dedication and the Anointings

The heart of the entire order of service is the dedication of the church and the altar. The revised ceremony has simplified and reordered the traditional parts, making it flow more logically, leading up to the celebration of the first Liturgy of the Eucharist in the new space.

91. Schemata 370, n. 33.
92. Eusebius, *The History of the Church*, trans. G. A. Williamson (New York: Penguin Books, 1983), X:4, pp. 383–401.
93. Schemata 370, n. 34.

The Litany of Supplication

The third part of the ceremony opens with the litany. This makes sense within the liturgy, as it falls where the universal prayer normally takes place, and it leads to the main ritual action. The relocation of the litany to this stage of the ceremony, however, altered the tradition. The litany used to accompany the procession from outside to inside the building, in sequence with the sprinkling of blessed water. Now both elements have been repurposed: the sprinkling occurs inside the building at the moment that replaces the penitential act, and the litany follows the Liturgy of the Word to prepare for the prayers of blessing. The litany occupies a similar location in other rituals of the Catholic Church, such as the baptism of adults and the ordination of priests, thus bringing greater harmony among them all.

The bishop invites the people to join him in prayer. The deacon invites all to kneel unless the dedication is taking place on a Sunday or on any weekday in Easter Time. This continues an ancient custom in the church that advocated standing for prayer to express one's faith in the resurrection and therefore forbade kneeling throughout the fifty days of Easter. The bishop concludes the litany with a prayer (ODCA II:57–60 and CB 899).

The earliest records of the rite of dedication included a singing of a litany. The ninth century Ordo XLI has the clergy enter the building to a litany and prostrate themselves before the altar.[94] Even the 1961 pontifical had kept the litany within the first part of the ceremony at the entrance to the church.[95] Its retention honored one of the most ancient and consistent parts of the dedication ceremony.

---

94. Ordo XLI 3, p. 340.
95. PR 1961, pp. 131–34.

The revisers knew of this tradition, but they had already recommended Psalm 24 for entering the new building. Calabuig says that they considered two options pertaining to the litany: "either to omit it completely or to insert it organically and in a liturgically valid way into another moment of the rite. The second alternative was chosen."[96] This preserved the integrity of the newly crafted entrance to the church, placed the litany where people encountered it in other rituals, and located the listing of the saints close to the upcoming optional deposition of the relics.

The bishop's introduction is a new composition, having no precedent in the history of the rite, and he has freedom to use these or similar words. He invites the people to pray to God, "who makes the hearts of the faithful into spiritual temples for himself" (ODCA II:57). Immediately, one can see the concern of the revisers to draw attention not only to the church building but to the people who are the church. The first draft created a simpler formula: "Dearly beloved, let us pray that the supplication of the saints, our brothers and sisters, may help us who are dedicating this church to God."[97] The second draft enriched this to almost exactly the formula that remained in the ODCA.[98]

The second draft gave a complete listing of saints, almost identical to what appears in the litany today.[99] It had Joseph preceding John the Baptist, whereas John now takes the prior position. This may have been an oversight because John preceded Joseph in the 1961 pontifical.[100] That same pontifical had

96. Calabuig, "Commentary," p. 18.
97. Schemata 370, n. 35.
98. Schemata 375, n. 34, p. 9.
99. Schemata 375, n. 36, pp. 9–10.
100. PR 1961, p. 132.

a more complex opening, calling upon the Trinity and upon Mary under various titles. It named summary groups, such as angels and archangels, patriarchs and prophets, apostles and evangelists, the disciples, popes and confessors, priests and deacons, monks and hermits, and virgins and widows. Mary Magdalene had been listed among the women near the end, but she has been relocated among the apostles. Ignatius of Antioch and Athanasius were added to the second postconciliar draft; Vincent and Sylvester were omitted. Anthony was removed, whereas Basil and Martin were added. Francis and Dominic were listed individually in 1961, but they became paired after the council. Francis Xavier, John Mary Vianney, Catherine of Siena, and Teresa of Avila were all added, and Cecilia, Agatha, and Anastasia, who are all still optional in the first eucharistic prayer, were removed from the revised litany. Anastasia had just been restored to the litany in 1961, "so as to have a representative of the Holy Widows."[101] Agatha had been listed before Agnes in the past and was moved after Cecilia for the 1961 revision.[102] Of these, only Agnes's name survived the final revision, and she was moved to a place among the martyrs, along with the newly added Perpetua and Felicity.

In the next part of the litany, many of the petitions were eliminated or redrafted. Durandus had added a petition near the conclusion: "That you may be pleased to bless this church and this altar, consecrating them to your honor and to the name of Saint N. Lord, we ask you, hear our prayer." The bishop repeated the petition while elaborating the verb, "to bless and sanctify," and then said the petition a third time with a yet more expanded verb: "to bless, sanctify and consecrate."[103] The same

---

101. Giampietro, *Development of the Liturgical Reform*, p. 305, n. 1068.
102. Giampietro, p. 308, n. 1110.
103. Durand II:II, 44, p. 463.

threefold petition reappeared through the 1961 revision,[104] even though it had come up for discussion. At a meeting in 1958, "As in the past, it was asked that the invocation '*Ut ecclesiam et altare hoc*' be repeated three times since this was a solemn moment."[105] In the postconciliar edition of the ODCA, however, the petition was simplified, its repetitions eliminated, and it was reassigned from the bishop to the singers leading the litany: "Consecrate this church for your worship." The name of the patron saint, which used to appear in this petition, may be added elsewhere: in the proper location among the entire list of saints—a martyr with martyrs, a virgin among virgins, for example.

The concluding prayer is a new composition that alludes both to Jesus' conversation with Zacchaeus (Luke 19:9) and to part of the conversation between Jesus and the woman at the well (John 4:23). The bishop prays that the building may be a "house of salvation" and of grace, where Christians "will worship you in spirit and in truth" (ODCA II:60).

The first draft of this oration took a different direction. The bishop was to say, "Mercifully accept our prayers, O Lord, at the intercession of your Saints, so that this place may become exalted by your indwelling, and your people may always receive new increase."[106] The second draft changed it to the prayer in force today, which only adds to it the name of the Blessed Virgin Mary.[107]

When ICEL drafted its translation, it preferred the expression "at the intercession" of the Blessed Virgin Mary, not "through the intercession." That would have been more faithful to the

104. PR 1961, pp. 133–34.
105. Giampietro, *Development of the Liturgical Reform*, p. 305, n. 1069.
106. Schemata 370, n. 39.
107. Schemata 375, n. 37, p. 10.

Latin and would have preserved a theological point: The church does not tell God how to answer its prayers ("grant this through her") but reminds God who stands with the church at prayer ("grant this as Mary too is requesting it.)"

The Deposition of the Relics

Relics of martyrs or of other saints may be set into place "under the altar" inside a previously prepared opening.[108] The relics of any saint may be used, but the relics of martyrs are preferred, in order "to signify that the sacrifice of the members has drawn its origin from the Sacrifice of the Head" (ODCA II:12).

Missteps are to be avoided. The relics are now to be of a sufficient size to be recognized as parts of human bodies. This discourages the placement of excessively small relics of one or more saints beneath the altar. If the relics cannot be authenticated, an altar is dedicated without them (ODCA II:5ab and CB 866ab).

Because the earlier practice insisted on securing the relics of martyrs alone, the committee first discussing the renewal of the dedication rite in 1965 asked whether it was not better to have the authentic relics of a confessor than the dubious relics of a martyr.[109] Shortly thereafter, the Roman Missal enshrined the approved use of relics of non-martyr saints (GIRM, p. 266 in the first edition, p. 302 in the third).[110]

A reliquary must not be placed on top of the altar or inside the mensa (ODCA II:5c and CB 866c), the top reserved for contact with the vessels holding the Body and Blood of

---

108. For a deeper study of the practice, see Suzanne Sarah Herold, "Christ and the Triumphant Victims: Relics and the Altar in the *Ordo dedicationis ecclesiae et altaris*" (PhD diss., The Catholic University of America, 2016).

109. Schemata 65, I:5a, p. 3.

110. Schemata 370, III:2b.

Christ during the celebration of the Eucharist. Placing relics in the mensa had been the custom in the past, but it has now been revoked. The altar should clearly signify Christ, not the saints. In the words of St. Augustine, "It is not to any of the martyrs, but to the God of the martyrs, though in memory of the martyrs, that we raise our altars."[111] To this point, "In new churches, statues and pictures of saints may not be placed above the altar" (CB 921). The *Ceremonial of Bishops* clarifies further: "In places where altars are customarily dedicated to God in honor of the saints, the practice may be continued, but it should be made clear to the people that the altar is dedicated to God alone" (921).

Some people still mistakenly hold that the ministers who kiss the altar at the beginning and end of Mass are kissing the relics of saints. They are not. They are kissing the altar, which symbolizes Christ.

If the community held a prayer vigil the night before, the relics have already been set apart and venerated. If the dedication Mass began outdoors, the relics have been carried and set in a temporary place of honor. If the liturgy began indoors, they already occupy that place. If these are relics of martyrs, any deacons who carry them wear a red stole and preferably a dalmatic. If they carry the relics of other saints, deacons wear white. If priests carry the relics, they wear chasubles of the appropriate color. If lay people carry the relics, they wear albs or other suitable vesture (ODCA II:24a and CB 876a).

At the conclusion of the Litany of Supplication, the bishop approaches the altar, a deacon or priest carries the relics in procession toward him, and he places them in the opening. All may sing Psalm 15 with the antiphon "Beneath the altar of

---

111. Augustine, *Contra Faustum* XX, 21: *Patrologia Latina* 42, 384, cited in CB 921.

God you have been placed, O Saints of God: intercede for us before the Lord Jesus Christ," or "The bodies of the Saints are buried in peace and their names will live for all eternity." In Easter Time, that second recommended antiphon concludes with an Alleluia. A stonemason closes the aperture, and the bishop returns to his chair (ODCA II:61 and CB 900).

According to the New Testament, the witness of martyrs began spreading the Gospel almost immediately after the death and resurrection of Christ. In Acts of the Apostles, Luke relates the stoning of Stephen in terms redolent of the crucifixion of Jesus. In their trials both had false witnesses brought against them (Acts 6:11 and Matt 26:59), they were accused of blasphemy (Acts 6:13 and Matt 26:65), and they prayed for the forgiveness of their killers (Acts 7:60 and Luke 23:34). From the beginning, discipleship demanded the kind of Christ-inspired commitment that could lead to one's death.

A footnote in ODCA II:12 cites Revelation 6:9: "I saw underneath the altar the souls of those who had been slaughtered for the Word of God and for the witness they had given." John the elder saw this chilling vision at the breaking of the fifth seal. The slaughtered souls ask how long it will be before God avenges their blood, and they are told "to be patient a little while longer until the number was filled of their fellow servants and brothers [and sisters] who were going to be killed as they had been" (Rev 6:9-11). Thus, the presence of the relics of martyrs beneath the altar of a local parish church pulls the community into the Bible's sobering vision of hard-won places at the altar of God's heavenly dwelling.

Early Christians sometimes celebrated the Eucharist at the tombs of the saints. Cyprian of Carthage (+258) "tells of the Eucharist being celebrated at grave sites (Epistles 39:3; 12:3)." At that time, altars did not yet enclose tombs; the faithful probably brought some portable altar for the celebration. In Rome, however, altars were built quite early over the tombs of Sts. Peter and Paul.[112]

In 386, Ambrose sent his sister Marcella a copy of the sermon he had preached when placing the relics of Sts. Gervase and Protase under an altar.[113] This followed the people's aforementioned vigil over the relics. Ambrose explained, "Let the triumphant victims be brought to the place where Christ is the victim. But he upon the altar, who suffered for all; they under the altar, who were redeemed by his passion."[114] This early reference to the bodies of martyrs "under" the altar supports the present practice.

Pope Vigilius's sixth-century letter to Profuturus, referenced above, confirmed the practice of placing relics of the martyrs under the altar but did not require it, "for we know that the consecration of any church in which no shrine [= relics of the martyrs] is included, is accomplished simply by the celebration of Masses."[115] Thus, in his day, the Eucharist alone consecrated a church that had no relics.

The eighth-century Gelasian Sacramentary retains an announcement that a bishop could make in order to comfort those churches that possessed only some parts rather than the entire body of a saint:

> Beloved brothers and sisters, among the solemnities of the virtuous saints, which pertain to the glory of Christ our Lord, there stands out especially that of the martyrs, who, having

112. R. X. Redmond, F. Kraus, and Fr. R. McManus, "Altar in Christian Liturgy: In the Liturgy," *New Catholic Encyclopedia*, 2nd ed. (Detroit: Thomson Gale, 2003).

113. Jounel, *Church at Prayer*, I:217.

114. Ambrose, Letter XXII:13. Author's translation of Latin from Chengalikavil, "Dedicazione della chiesa," p. 71.

115. Vigilius, Letter 4, cited by Calabuig, "Rite," p. 340.

accepted death through the confession of his name, were able to receive a heavenly prize, so that as their resplendent relics were set in place for the prayers of the faithful, the whole body of the saint is believed to be present.[116]

The same sacramentary assigned this secret to the Mass celebrated on the day devoted to the martyred Saints Cosmas and Damian, then as now observed on September 26: "In honor of the precious death of your just ones, O Lord, we come to offer that sacrifice from which all martyrdom draws its origin. Through Christ our Lord." That prayer now appears in the Missal as the first option for the prayer over the offerings within the common of several martyrs in Easter Time. It alludes to the aforementioned sermon of St. Ambrose, who drew a connection between the sufferings of Christ, whom the altar symbolizes, and the sufferings of the martyrs placed beneath it.

Paragraph II:12 from the ODCA footnotes this prayer, St. Ambrose, and Revelation to explain the custom of placing the relics of saints beneath altars. A later chapter of the ODCA cites the same references to Ambrose and Revelation after this preliminary remark:

> It is not, then, the bodies of the Martyrs that give honor to the altar; but rather it is the altar that renders the burial place of the Martyrs worthy of honor. For to honor the bodies of the Martyrs and other Saints and to signify that the sacrifice of the members has its source in the Sacrifice of the Head, it is fitting for altars to be constructed over their tombs, or for their relics to be placed under altars (IV:5).

By the ninth century, the deposition of relics in an altar had been sufficiently formalized to take its place among other early

---

116. Gelasian Sacramentary, 805.

Roman rites.[117] The bishop was to conduct the ceremony, one of many that completely preceded the celebration of the Eucharist. He prepared exorcized water, added chrism to some of it, and made a cement. He "baptized" the altar with more of the same water. As the relics were brought forward, the schola sang a litany. The bishop offered a prayer, received the relics from a priest, and set them on the new altar. The bishop anointed the four corners of the aperture with chrism, inserted three particles of the consecrated Body of the Lord along with three grains of incense, and placed the relics into the same opening. Meanwhile, all sang the Revelation-inspired antiphon that has survived from the ninth century through the contemporary rite with only minor changes: "Beneath the altar of the Lord you have been placed: intercede for us through the one by whom you have been made worthy." The bishop offered another prayer and sealed the relics inside with the cement he had prepared.[118]

Similar ceremonies can be found in other sources, such as the tenth-century Roman-Germanic Pontifical[119] and the twelfth-century Roman Pontifical.[120] By the thirteenth century, Durandus accounted for the possibility that the church had no relics, instructing the bishop to enclose particles of the consecrated Body of the Lord as the alternative.[121] The prayer that concluded this ceremony for over a thousand years remained in the 1961 pontifical at the expressed desire of the committee

---

117. Ordo XLIII, pp. 411–13.

118. Ordo XLII:4–14, pp. 398–401.

119. *Le Pontifical Romano-Germanique du Dixième Siècle* (PRG), ed. Cyrille Vogel and Reinhard Elze, Studi e Testi 226 (Vatican City: Biblioteca Apostolica Vaticana 1963), XXXIII:37a–45, p. 88.

120. *Pontifical romain au Moyen Âge, Tome I, XII*, XVII:48–53, pp. 186–88.

121. Durand II:II, 3, p. 456.

preparing it,[122] but that was its last appearance. It read, "O God, who from each model of the saints fashion an eternal dwelling place for you, grant heavenly increases to your building: and may we always be helped by the rewards of those whose relics we enclose here by devout custom. Through Christ our Lord."[123] That closing prayer, which pertained more to the building and relics, ceded its place to the more important prayer of dedication, soon to be recited over the place and the people.

Luke Chengalikavil notes that the placement of relics under the altar exemplifies the proper reverence due to the martyrs, expressed in the council's Constitution on the Sacred Liturgy:[124] "By celebrating the days on which they died, the church proclaims the paschal mystery in the saints who have suffered and have been glorified with Christ" (104).[125]

The first draft of the postconciliar rite had the deacons and priests bring the relics to the bishop as the litany was just beginning, after the invocation of Holy Mary, Mother of God.[126] The idea did not survive even the second draft, so the final version has the relics come after the litany has completely concluded.

The traditional refrain, "Beneath the altar of God," draws its inspiration from Revelation 6:9. An expanded version of the antiphon made that clear in the 1961 pontifical.[127] From the sixteenth century, though, this versicle from Psalm 149:5 had been joined to the antiphon: "Let the faithful exult in glory, and rejoice as they take their rest." Thus, one verse from the

---

122. Giampietro, *Development of the Liturgical Reform*, p. 305, n. 1075.

123. PR 1961, p. 146.

124. Chengalikavil, "Dedicazione della chiesa," p. 81.

125. Austin Flannery, ed., *Vatican Council II: Constitutions, Decrees, Declarations; The Basic Sixteen Documents* (Collegeville, MN: Liturgical Press, 2014), p. 150.

126. Schemata 370, n. 38.

127. PR 1961, p. 145.

psalms served as a prophecy for the final resting place of the relics of the saints.[128]

In the postconciliar reform, however, Psalm 15, which asks, "Lord, who may abide in your tent, and dwell on your holy mountain?," replaces Psalm 149:5. Calabuig notes that the choice probably signifies the meaning of the deposition of the relics, "the resting place of mortal remains in a dwelling place of holiness and peace, the eucharistic altar. As well it is a sign of the martyrs' entry, following upon a heroic following of Christ, into the 'tent' of the Lord, their resting place on the holy mountain where they will enjoy eternal rest."[129]

A record of the dedication of the church detailing the date, the name of the bishop, the name of the church, and the names of the martyrs or saints in the reliquary is be signed in triplicate by the bishop, the rector, and representatives of the local community. One of these copies is kept in the diocesan archives, a second in the parish archives. The third may be sealed inside the reliquary (ODCA II:25). The ritual does not explain when this happens. The record could be set inside the altar's aperture before the ceremony begins, or it may be carried to its place after the Litany of the Saints either before the deposition of relics or even after the deposition of relics, just before the opening is sealed.

The entire relics ceremony is optional. Mass may be regularly celebrated in a church on an altar that does not have relics of saints enclosed.

The Prayer of Dedication

The bishop offers the prayer of dedication, one of the central components of the entire ceremony. He stands at either the

---

128. PR 1595–1596, p. 365.
129. Calabuig, "Commentary," p. 23.

chair or the altar. He praises God and acclaims the holiness of
the church, and then he asks God to pour sanctifying power
upon the church and its altar (ODCA II:62 and CB 901). The
introduction notes, "The celebration of the Eucharist is the
most important rite, and the only necessary one, for the dedication of a church" (ODCA II:15). Still, tradition calls for a
special prayer that dedicates the building to the Lord and im-
plores his blessing.

The Old Testament antecedent for such a prayer is Solomon's at the dedication of the temple he had constructed in
Jerusalem (1 Kgs 8:23-53). Standing before the altar, with his
arms stretched toward heaven, Solomon recalled the wonders
that God had done (23-24), asked the Lord to be faithful to
the promise of a dynasty (25), and requested "that your eyes
may be open night and day toward this house" (29).[130] Some
of these sentiments are repeated in the eighth-century Gelasian Sacramentary's example of a dedication prayer: "Hear the
prayers of your servants, and may your eyes be open upon this
house day and night."[131]

The tenth-century Roman-Germanic Pontifical presented
an eloquent prayer for blessing the church. The bishop begged
the eternal God to be present to those seeking mercy:

> May your Holy Spirit, overflowing with the richness of sev-
> enfold grace, descend also upon this your church, which we,
> though unworthy, consecrate under the invocation of your
> holy name in honor of the holy cross on which your Son, our
> Lord Jesus Christ, coeternal to you, was pleased to suffer for
> the redemption of the world, and [in honor] of your holy
> martyr N., so that whenever your holy name will be invoked

---

130. Cesare Giraudo, *La struttura letteraria della Preghiera Eucaristica*
(Rome: Biblical Institute Press, 1982), pp. 150–53.

131. Gelasian Sacramentary, 690.

in this your house, the prayers of those who will have called out to you may be heard by you, the loving Lord.[132]

This prayer, which the previous ritual books traditionally called a "preface," goes on to ask that the church become a place where "the sick are healed, the weak recuperate, the disabled are cured, lepers are cleansed, the blind receive sight, and demons are driven out."[133]

The 1595–1596 Pontifical turned to the Gelasian for inspiration. The bishop offered a prayer that recalled Solomon's, asking that God's "eyes be opened upon this house day and night."[134]

As this ritual was being revised in 1958, the committee wanted the formula for this consecration of a church and altar to include "the Saint to whom the church is dedicated," with the words "in honor of God and in memory of St. N."[135] Members also requested a simplification of the formula in which the bishop addressed the door of the church: "Door, be consecrated and entrusted to the Lord God; door, be the gateway of peace, through him who called himself the gate, Jesus Christ our Lord."[136] These changes were accepted for the 1961 pontifical,[137] but they did not endure through the postconciliar revision, which kept the dedication prayer focused on Christ and the church. Along with similar liturgical changes affecting ceremonies such as the blessing of incense and the consecration of chrism, the post–Vatican II liturgy eliminates the custom of having the presider address created things.

132. PRG XL:48.
133. PRG XL:48.
134. Pontifical 1595–1596, p. 339.
135. Giampietro, *Development of the Liturgical Reform*, pp. 305–6, n. 1076.
136. Giampietro, p. 306, n. 1077.
137. PR 1961, pp. 146 and 148.

Traditionally, this liturgy included two prayers, both called prefaces, one for the altar and another for the church. In 1965, the first gathering of the committee to reform the rites took note of this and questioned the value of this "double preface in one and the same rite."[138] The first draft actually asked if a prayer of dedication was needed at all because of the celebration of the Eucharist. "Is it agreeable that the preface of the Mass replace the consecration prayer; indeed, to omit the consecration prayer?"[139] In the end, the ceremony preserves a single prayer, no longer called a preface, that asks a blessing on both church and altar, although the bishop offers a secondary prayer later when he anoints the altar.

The prayer of dedication is a new composition. It drew some inspiration from the preface for the dedication of a church in the Ambrosian Rite, which says in part, "the faithful are chosen stones, enlivened by the Spirit and sealed by charity, the apostles being the foundation, and [Christ] the cornerstone."[140]

An introductory declaration sets the context for the dedication of a place where people will be "instructed by the word" and "nourished by the Sacraments." The bishop makes multiple statements showing the relationship between the physical building and the people of God. He then explicitly expresses the purpose of the prayer, asking the Lord, "graciously pour forth from heaven your sanctifying power upon this church and this altar, to make this for ever a holy place with a table always prepared for the Sacrifice of Christ" (ODCA II:62). The bishop lists the effects of the prayer: the faithful will celebrate the Eucharist, praise will resound, the poor will find mercy, the

---

138. Schemata 67, I:4d, p. 2.

139. Schemata 370, Question 2, p. V.

140. Prefazio, Comune della dedicazione della chiesa, *Messale ambrosiano quotidiano IV, Per le celebrazioni dei santi*, p. 1182.

oppressed secure true freedom, and all will be clothed with the dignity of God's children. This conclusion imitates the style of the one from the Roman-Germanic Pontifical. Oddly missing is the explicit epiclesis noted above from the same pontifical, "May your Holy Spirit . . . descend also upon this your holy church."

Relying on multiple biblical allusions, the bishop calls the church the "glorious Bride" of Christ (Rev 21:2), "the chosen vine of the Lord" (John 15:5), "a holy temple" (1 Peter 2:5) "standing upon the foundation of the Apostles with Christ Jesus its chief cornerstone" (Eph 2:20), and "a City set high on a mountain for all to see" (Matt 5:14), resplendent "with the unfading light of the Lamb" (Rev 21:23). The dedication will make this a place where people "being dead to sin, may be reborn to heavenly life" (Rom 6:11) and from which "they come exultant to the Jerusalem which is above" (Rev 21:22-23). The cascade of images reaches deeply into the Word of God to dedicate a space in which that Word will resound.

The Anointing of the Altar and the Walls of the Church
Next begins a series of symbolic actions that "express in visible signs several aspects of that invisible work which the Lord accomplishes through the Church in the celebration of the divine mysteries, especially the Eucharist" (ODCA II:16). The altar and walls are anointed, incense is burned, the altar is covered with its cloth, and the candles are lighted.[141]

By the anointing with chrism, the altar is made a symbol of Christ who, before all others, is and is called, "The Anointed One." Indeed, Christ offered the sacrifice of his life for the

---

141. For a deeper study, see James Michael Starke, "The Spirit Dwells Here: A Liturgical Theology of the Anointing in *Ordo dedicationis ecclesiae et altaris*" (PhD diss., The Catholic University of America, 2018).

salvation of all on the altar of his Body. Paul explained to the Corinthians that Moses received water in the desert from a rock that was Christ (1 Cor 10:4); Ambrose of Milan called the altar one form of the body of Christ.[142]

The anointing of the walls of the church "signifies that it is given over entirely and perpetually to Christian worship" (ODCA II:16a). Calabuig notes that St. Peter calls Christians living stones of a spiritual house (1 Pet 2:5). "As the Head was anointed with the Spirit, so are the members in the sacraments; as the altar was anointed, so are the stones."[143]

The bishop prepares to anoint the altar by putting on the gremial, a linen apron. He may either remove his chasuble first or wear the gremial over it (ODCA II:63 and CB 902). This apron protects a bishop's vestments on other occasions that call for a generous use of chrism, such as the ordination of priests and bishops.

Assisting ministers accompany the bishop to the altar. Traditionally, a deacon presents the chrism to him. The bishop says, "May the Lord by his power sanctify this altar and this house, which by our ministry we anoint, so that as visible signs they may express the mystery of Christ and the Church" (ODCA II:64 and CB 903). As in the prayer of dedication, the bishop prays over the altar and the building, both of which are about to be anointed. He pours chrism on top of the altar, first in the middle, and then on the four corners. "It is praiseworthy for him to anoint the entire table with it." The image of their bishop spreading sacred chrism all across the top of their new altar is a memory that many participants in this ritual will hold for the rest of their lives.

---

142. Calabuig, "Commentary," p. 25.
143. Calabuig, p. 26.

Without any further spoken prayer, the anointing of the walls follows immediately. The bishop performs this action himself, or he may enlist the assistance of two or four priests, or he may entrust the anointing of the walls entirely to those priests (ODCA II:64 and CB 902 and 903). It is fitting that these be the concelebrants who will care for the community after the dedication (ODCA II:9 and CB 869). If priests assist, they receive their vessels of chrism from the hands of the bishop. They trace chrism onto the walls in four or twelve places in the form of a cross. Twelve crosses would be "in accordance with liturgical tradition," and four would signify "that the church is an image of the holy city of Jerusalem" (ODCA II:16a), recalling the twelve gates of the heavenly Jerusalem as seen by John, three facing each of the four directions (Rev 21:12-14).

Calabuig notes that the optional inclusion of priests to anoint is an innovation to the rite. "However, the option should be chosen for, in addition to shortening a long liturgy, it underlines the ecclesial meaning of the rite."[144]

Traditionally, the walls have been previously marked with crosses of stone, bronze, or other material, or they have been carved directly into the walls. A bracket beneath each cross is to be fit with a holder and candle to be lighted later. The crosses are to be distributed "at a convenient height" to facilitate access to them (ODCA II:22 and CB 874).

As the anointing takes place, all may sing (ODCA II:64 and CB 903). Psalm 84 is suggested because it first resounded when pilgrims arrived at the Jerusalem temple, extolling the building's loveliness and expressing the singers' yearning for it. Two antiphons are recommended: "Behold God's dwelling with the human race. He will live with them and they will be his people, and God himself with them will be their God," which is drawn

144. Calabuig, p. 27.

from Revelation 21:3, concluding with an "Alleluia" during Easter Time. Or "Holy is the temple of the Lord, God's own structure, God's own building," taken from 1 Corinthians 3:9.

After the anointing, the bishop returns to the chair, washes his hands, and removes his gremial. Any priests who assisted also wash their hands (ODCA II:65 and CB 904). Traditionally, ministers approach the bishop with a basin and pitcher of water, along with a lemon, cut across its equator and seeded, to remove the oil. Because of the sacredness of the chrism, the ministers fittingly pour this used water down the sacrarium in the sacristy.

The anointing of an altar recalls Jacob's actions after seeing in a dream a stairway that joined heaven and earth: He set up a memorial stone and poured oil on top of it (Gen 28:18). Altars of incense and of burnt offerings are among the items that God commanded Moses to consecrate (Exod 30:27-28 and Exod 40:10). Leaders of ancient Israel presented offerings on the occasion of an altar's dedication (Num 7:10-11, 84 and 88).

Several early Christian sources list altars among the destinations for sacred oil: the fourth-century deacon Ephrem the Syrian, the fifth-century Testament of the Lord, and the sixth-century work of Pseudo-Dionysius. In the West, Caesarius of Arles presided at the Council of Agde in 506, which decreed, "It has been decided that altars should be consecrated not only by anointing with chrism but also by a [bishop's] blessing." In 517, the Council of Epaone declared, "Altars are not to be consecrated by anointing with chrism unless they are made of stone." Isidore presided over the Second Council of Seville in 619, which decreed that priests may not perform certain actions reserved for bishops, such as ordinations, "nor may they licitly consecrate a church or an altar."[145]

---

145. Calabuig, "Rite," p. 343.

The practice of anointing altars reached Rome by the ninth century. The bishop first poured blessed water on the altar, then chrism, amid the singing of psalms and offering of prayers; one of those was Psalm 84.[146] In another order of service, after the bishop had placed the relics within the altar, he poured chrism on the four corners of the mensa.[147]

In the tenth century, the bishop still poured oil on the four corners of the altar top amid prayers and psalms, including Psalm 84,[148] but he received an additional instruction: "And using his hand, he anoints that entire altar with holy oil, while another priest continually carries incense around that altar."[149]

By the thirteenth century, the bishop was given words to say while making the sign of the cross three times: "May this altar be sanctified in the name of the Father and of the Son and of the Holy Spirit."[150] Durandus altered the formula in the same century, removing its reference to the Trinity and inserting the patron of the church among the saints: "May this altar be sanctified in honor of God and of the glorious virgin Mary and of all the saints, and to the name and memory of Saint N."[151]

By the sixteenth century, the bishop first poured water onto the altar's four corners and middle, and then he anointed the same five places with the oil of catechumens before anointing them all again with chrism. He no longer spread the oil over the entire top of the altar.[152]

---

146. Ordo XLI:17–18, p. 344, and 21, p. 345.

147. Ordo XLII:15, p. 401.

148. PRG XXXIII:22–24, p. 85.

149. PRG XL:52–53, p. 144.

150. *Le Pontifical Romain au Moyen-age, II. Le Pontifical de la Curie Romaine au XIII*Siècle*, Studi e Testi 87, ed. Michel Andrieu (Vatican City: Biblioteca Apostolica Vaticana, 1940), XXIII:39, p. 430.

151. Durand II II:68, p. 470.

152. PR 1595–1596, pp. 372 and 377.

Regarding the walls of the church, the tenth-century ritual called for the bishop to anoint the door and lintels as well.[153] He walked around the church clockwise, anointing the walls with twelve crosses, dipping his thumb in chrism each time. He recited these words: "May this temple be sanctified in the name of the Father and of the Son and of the Holy Spirit."[154]

In the sixteenth century, the bishop repeatedly dipped his thumb into chrism and anointed the walls on twelve places in the sign of a cross.[155] He scaled a ladder for each anointing, assistants repositioning it each time for him to mount again.[156] The rubrics now call for the crosses to be positioned at a convenient height (ODCA II:22 and CB 874); in the past, the height was not convenient.

Much of this was retained in the 1961 revision, though the bishop was to anoint the building first, then the altar. He no longer used the oil of catechumens. Other bishops could assist in anointing side altars.[157] The postconciliar revision restored the former sequence: the bishop anoints the altar before the walls. Calabuig notes, "anointing begins with the altar, symbol of Christ, and proceeds to the side walls, symbols of Christians, stones of the Church."[158] The erection of side altars has been discontinued in favor of a single altar for the celebration of Mass (See ODCA IV 6–7 and CB 919).

In 1965, as discussions for this revision were beginning, committee members wondered if anointing the door should remain with the circuit of anointing the walls as in 1961, or if they should reinstate a former practice of anointing the lintels

153. PRG XL:124, p. 168.
154. PRG XXXIII:27, p. 86.
155. PR 1595–1596, pp. 378–79.
156. A sketch appears in the edition of the 1595–1596 Pontifical, p. 384.
157. PR 1961 39–44, pp. 146–50.
158. Calabuig, "Commentary," p. 27.

toward the beginning of the celebration when the bishop was to carry the relics into the church.[159] In the end, the anointing of the door was removed from the dedication altogether. This put more focus on the twelve or four crosses on the walls, symbols of the new Jerusalem.

The 1965 committee also noted, "Some people lament the suppression of the rite of anointing the entire mensa with holy chrism; and they wonder therefore whether such an anointing could be again restored."[160] The first draft addressed this issue directly: "If it seems appropriate, the bishop may pour oil on the whole mensa of the altar."[161] This was to replace pouring chrism in crosses on the four corners and center of the altar. The committee questioned another practice that the ancient rituals had retained: "Why is sacred chrism dried off the walls [with a towel]?"[162] That practice was indeed eliminated.

The first draft crafted a prayer for the bishop to say just before anointing, and this has remained in place word for word.[163] The same draft had the bishop associate two or four priests with him to anoint twelve or four places on the walls; in the first drafts, the ministry of these priests was not optional.[164] The first draft proposed singing Psalm 86,[165] which was eventually replaced with Psalm 84. It also proposed the two antiphons that remain in ODCA II:64, as cited above. The draft of the first was lightly modified to accept the new Vulgate translation of Revelation 21:3. The second antiphon remains unchanged from the first draft.

159. Schemata 67, I:4a, p. 2.
160. Schemata 67, I:4c, p. 2.
161. Schemata 370, III:A2c.
162. Schemata 67, I:7c, p. 3.
163. Schemata 370, n. 41.
164. Schemata 370, Pars Tertia B40 and 42, and Schemata 375, p. 11, n. 39.
165. Schemata 370, Pars Tertia B43.

All of this produced a leaner, more expressive ceremony showing the connection between the altar and the walls of the new building both in the prayer of dedication and in the action of anointing. It also clarified the purposes of devotion: It dedicated the building to God.

The Incensation of the Altar and the Church

Symbolic actions reverencing the altar and church continue. "*Incense* is burned on the altar to signify that the Sacrifice of Christ, which is there perpetuated in mystery, ascends to God as a pleasing fragrance; this is also a sign that the pleasing and acceptable prayers of the faithful rise up to the throne of God" (ODCA II:16).

The ceremony recalls the altar that Noah built when the floodwaters subsided and from which the sacrifice he offered released an aroma that pleased God (Gen 8:20-21). Among the commands that the Lord spoke to Moses were to offer a sweet-smelling oblation (Exod 29:41 and Num 28:3-10) and to create an altar of incense (Exod 30:1-9, 34-38, and 37:25-29).[166]

Either a brazier of hot coals or a heap of incense mixed with tapers is set upon the altar. The bishop lights it, releasing smoke and aromas. The first of these options is clearer, but the second simplifies the preconciliar practice:

> Then the bishop sprinkles the altar with blessed water and, having put on the miter, uses his own hand to form five crosses out of incense, each of the five [aligning] the grains upon those five places of the altar on which the crosses of water, oil [of catechumens] and chrism had been made earlier; and upon each cross of incense he puts one cross made from tapers, measured to match the cross made from the

---

166. Chengalikavil, "Dedicazione della chiesa," p. 83.

grains of incense; and the wicks of each cross are lighted, so that with them the incense may catch fire and burn. When all the crosses have been lighted, the bishop, his miter having been removed, kneels before the altar, and the choir immediately begins, "*Veni, Sancte Spiritus.*"[167]

Calabuig notes,

> For many centuries, down to our day, the most moving part of the entire rite was the blessing of the incense. On five points of the altar signed with holy chrism there burned five crosses made of wax and grains of incense. The altar became a field of fire from which arose dense clouds of smoke and fragrant balsam. During this the schola sang the solemn *Veni, Sancte Spiritus* while the entire assembly—clergy and laity—remained kneeling, listening intently to the singing, in silent prayer.[168]

This ceremony has been simplified partly because "it tended to make the faithful erroneously believe that this part was the culminating point of the entire celebration."[169] The solemn invocation of the Spirit and the kneeling of the assembly were removed. The new texts and the incensation of the people widened the meaning of this ritual to a fuller commemoration of the new covenant in Christ.

The first draft of the liturgy explained the separation of two elements of the former rite, the fire and the incense:

> The *Rite of Incense* of the former Order has been changed slightly into a rite of incense and fire; for the incense, which burned on the altar, grew into a flame. In the new Order,

167. PR 1595–1596, p. 386.
168. Calabuig, "Commentary," p. 29.
169. Calabuig, p. 29.

the rites of incense and fire have been separated: the church is illumined with candles and all the [electrical] lamps; incense is diffused on the altar, the people, and the walls of the church.[170]

The bishop prays, starting with an allusion to Psalm 141:2, and continuing with a reference to 2 Corinthians 2:14-15 and Ephesians 5:2, "Let our prayer rise, O Lord, like incense in your sight; and as this house is filled with a pleasing fragrance, so let your Church be fragrant with the aroma of Christ" (ODCA II:66 and CB 905). ICEL had some discussion on this translation because two different words in Latin sound rather similar in English: "fragrance" and "fragrant." The committee tried some other renderings, such as "sweet perfume" for the first occurrence and "redolent" for the second. Neither seemed to work. Because "fragrance" has a larger framework than "perfumes"—flowers, for example, have a fragrance but not perfume—no change was made.

The bishop adds incense to several thuribles. One minister incenses him at the chair, while other ministers incense the people and the walls of the building (ODCA II:67 and CB 905).

"Moreover, the incensation of the main body of the church indicates that the dedication makes it a house of prayer, but the People of God are incensed first, for they are the living temple in which each faithful member is a spiritual altar" (ODCA II:16). The interpretation alludes to Romans 12:1, where Paul asks his readers to make their bodies a holy and living sacrifice, acceptable to God.

The first draft had made this incensation optional and had placed it *after* the lighting of the candles of the church: "If it seems appropriate, the bishop also puts incense in other

170. Schemata 370, III:A2d.

censers, with which ministers will incense the people and the nave of the church."[171] It then had the bishop incense the altar and the cross, as at Mass. Both of the first drafts had suggested enthroning the lectionary after the readings. If that had been done, ministers incensed the lectionary on its stand before taking thuribles and passing through the church to incense the people and the walls.[172] Placing the incensation as the last of the symbolic actions put it closer to its more ordinary usage during the preparation of the gifts.

The second draft still had the incensation follow the lighting of the church, but it expanded the ceremony at the altar:

> When the rite of Lighting has been completed, a brazier for burning aromatics is placed near the altar or upon it, or, if desired, a heap of incense mixed with candles is made upon the altar, which may more easily be burned and send out sharper flames. The bishop puts incense into the brazier, or after a minister has handed him a taper, he lights the heap of incense.[173]

These instructions led to the options that remain in the ODCA for the objects set upon the altar: either a brazier of hot coals or a heap of incense mixed with tapers. The incensation relates more to the dedication of the altar than to the preparation of the gifts; therefore, the lighting of altar candles was deferred to keep the incensation closer to the dedicatory prayer and anointing. The gifts of bread and wine are never incensed at this Mass.

During the incensation in the ODCA, all sing, and Psalm 138 is recommended with its refrain, "An Angel stood by the altar

171. Schemata 370, n. 46.
172. Schemata 370, n. 47, and Schemata 375, n. 46.
173. Schemata 375, n. 45, p. 13.

of the Temple holding in his hand a golden censer" (Rev 8:3),
or "In the presence of the Lord arose clouds of incense from
the hand of the Angel" (Rev 8:4). These two antiphons divide a
single one from the Latin chant repertoire, which is included in
its entirety as another option for the refrain. The elegant chant
features a melisma of thirty-eight notes on a single syllable of
the Latin word for "arose," as well as twenty-five notes on a
single syllable of the concluding "alleluia" (ODCA II:68 and
CB 905). The music aurally paints the airy rise of the smoke.

The 1961 pontifical had simplified the multiple antiphons of
the preconciliar rite. The group preparing the revision recommended adding a rubric that "one or more" of the antiphons
be sung.[174] This was indeed put into the pontifical just before
the council.[175]

Psalm 138 is new to the ceremony but blends well with the
passage from Revelation about the incense arising from the
angel's censer. It opens with the verses, "in the presence of the
angels I praise you. I bow down toward your holy temple."

In the first draft, the bishop concluded the incensation with
a prayer that the second draft moved later, after the covering
of the altar. It ultimately moved again to become the collect
(ODCA II:52).[176] Now no prayer concludes the incensation;
sufficient prayers apparently have been said.

The Covering of the Altar
Ministers may wipe the altar's mensa with cloths and then place
a nonporous linen over it. They cover this with the altar cloth
and may decorate the altar with flowers. They arrange candles
and, if necessary, a cross (ODCA II:69 and CB 906). The ritual

---

174. Giampietro, *Development of the Liturgical Reform*, p. 305, n. 1078.
175. PR 1961, p. 150.
176. Schemata 370, n. 49, and Schemata 375, n. 49, p. 14.

book places this action under the heading, "The Lighting of the Altar and the Church," but the introduction lists it separately, in keeping with the history of the rite.

"The *covering of the altar* indicates that the Christian altar is the altar of the Eucharistic Sacrifice and the table of the Lord. . . . For this reason the altar is prepared as the table of the sacrificial banquet and adorned as for a feast" (ODCA II:16c). The priests and the faithful stand around it to celebrate the sacrifice and eat the Lord's Supper. Its decoration shows that it is the Lord's table where the faithful are refreshed with the Body and Blood of Christ.

This is all that remains of what had been an elaborate ceremony for blessing altar cloths and vessels. As early as the ninth century, "While the subdeacons or acolytes hold the linens or all the other ornaments of the church, as well as whatever sacred vessels seem to pertain to the worship of God for the church, the bishop blesses [them], as is preserved in the Sacramentary."[177]

By the tenth century, the pontifical offered the bishop four prayers just to bless the altar cloths, and then additional prayers over linens and vessels held by subdeacons and acolytes.[178] After the bishop had set the relics in place, the blessed cloths were positioned over them and the altar.[179]

The accompanying prayers were kept in the ritual through the 1961 reform, and even the postconciliar drafts dedicated chapters to them. All that remains of these now is the blessing of a chalice and paten, which serves almost as an appendix in the final chapter of the entire Order (ODCA VII) and which

177. Ordo XLII:27, p. 346.
178. PRG XXXIII:31–35, pp. 86–87.
179. PRG XXXIII:36–46, pp. 87–89.

any priest may enact in a ceremony completely separate from the dedication of a church.

The purpose of wiping down the mensa is never explained. It had not been part of the drafts. Perhaps it relates to the option of burning a heap of incense with tapers on the altar (ODCA II:66). The debris would need to be wiped away. If the wiping removes excess chrism, prudence would call for actions afterwards in the sacristy: soaking those cloths in water that would then be poured down the sacrarium. The rubrics anticipate that some chrism remains on the altar top because a nonporous linen, something waterproof, is placed on top of the mensa and under the altar cloth. This protects the altar cloth from absorbing extra chrism, which properly belongs on the altar. If the mensa has been fashioned of wood rather than stone, it will absorb more of the oil.

At some church dedications, the parish sacristans who regularly tend the altar and its cloths conduct this part of the ceremony. It provides a rare moment when these parishioners, who labor behind the scenes of every Mass, may lovingly dress the altar in full view of the faithful whom they serve.

Flowers may be brought forward. The GIRM makes a clarification that the ODCA does not: "Floral decoration should always show moderation and be arranged around the altar rather than on the altar table" (GIRM 305). The dedication of the altar supplies an opportunity when less moderation may appropriately be shown; however, flowers belong around the altar, not on top of it, reserving the mensa for elements pertaining more directly to the sacred Eucharist.

For the dedication ceremony, those preparing the parish liturgy may assign the positioning of flowers to those parishioners who regularly decorate the church. This action honors the work that they do and places the careful arrangement of flowers in the hands of those with a trained eye for beauty.

Candlesticks and candles are brought forward. These "should be appropriately placed either on the altar or around it, according to the design of the altar and the sanctuary, so that the whole may be harmonious and the faithful may not be impeded from a clear view of what takes place at the altar or what is placed upon it" (GIRM 307). Unlike flowers, candles may be placed upon the altar; however, they should not block the view of the faithful from the actions taking place. The priest and the people gather around the same altar of sacrifice.

The cross is brought forward "if necessary." As the Missal indicates, "Likewise, either on the altar or near it, there is to be a cross, with the figure of Christ crucified upon it, a cross clearly visible to the assembled people. It is desirable that such a cross should remain near the altar even outside of liturgical celebrations, so as to call to mind for the faithful the saving Passion of the Lord" (GIRM 308). If the new church has a crucifix on the wall, it serves as the cross for each Mass, and no additional cross comes forward at this time. If the processional cross is used for the altar cross, it is now set in place. A cross had led the procession into the church (ODCA II:31, 37, and 43). Although the opening rubrics do not tell the crossbearer where to go, the cross was logically set aside inside the building; if it becomes the altar cross, the same crossbearer fittingly brings it forward.

Neither this rite nor the Missal makes provision for an additional cross to be placed upon the altar: the options are for a cross on the wall, the processional cross on its stand, or an altar cross in lieu of the other options. The Missal says, "on the altar or close to it, there is to be a cross adorned with a figure of Christ crucified" (GIRM 117), and "The cross adorned with a figure of Christ crucified, and carried in procession, may be placed next to the altar to serve as the altar cross, in which case it must be the only cross used; otherwise it is put away in a dignified place" (GIRM 122). The imagery works best if there is a single altar and a single cross to which it relates.

The Lighting of the Altar and the Church

The deacon steps forward, and the bishop hands him a small lighted candle, saying, "Let the light of Christ shine brightly in the church, that all nations may attain the fullness of truth." The bishop sits as the deacon lights the candles for the Eucharist (ODCA II:70 and CB 907).

All the other candles in the church are then lighted. The lighting is "a sign of rejoicing." The very rubrics acknowledge the joy in the hearts of the faithful. All may sing. The Canticle of Tobit is recommended with the antiphon, "Your light has come, Jerusalem: the glory of the Lord has risen upon you, and the nations will walk in your light, alleluia." During Lent, the antiphon becomes "Jerusalem, city of God, you will shine with splendid light, and all the ends of the earth will pay you homage" (ODCA II:71 and CB 907).

"The *lighting of the altar*, which is followed by the lighting of the church, reminds us that Christ is 'a light for revelation to the Gentiles,' whose brightness shines out in the Church and through her upon the whole human family" (ODCA II:16d). The explanation refers to Luke 2:32, where Simeon proclaims his prophecy about the infant child, an event commemorated each year in the church on February 2, when the liturgy begins with the blessing of candles. Simeon's prophecy also provides the gospel canticle for every Night Prayer in the Liturgy of the Hours. One may also think of John 8:12, where Jesus declares that he is the light of the world.

The rubrics do not explain how the bishop gets the lighted candle that he presents to the deacon, but logically, a different assisting minister hands it to him—not the deacon. Nor do the rubrics explain how the other candles are lighted, but any assisting ministers may perform this function. The candles set into the walls at the places of anointing shine for the first time. If the electrical lights have remained off, these may be illumined as well. The same Latin word for them, *lampadas*, appears in the rubrics of the Easter Vigil: these are the lights that have been off since the beginning of the Vigil and are switched on just before the singing of the *Exsultet*.[180]

The lighting of candles took place at different times in this liturgy throughout its history. For example, the first rubric of the first order of dedication recorded in the ninth century called for the lighting of candles: "For first, before the bishop may enter the church, twelve candles are lighted throughout the aisles of the church and [the clergy] put on sacred vestments."[181] By assigning both the lights and the vestments to the preliminaries, the rubric indicates that the church is "vested" even as the clergy are before the ritual begins.

The lengthy description of the entire ceremony in the tenth century carried the title, "What the Twelve Candles Mean."[182] The many pages that follow concern much more than that, but they begin by focusing on the lights that greet the clergy upon their arrival.[183] The commentary explains that the candles represent the twelve apostles, whose unified teaching adorns the church. The candles also recall the words of Christ, "You are the light of the world."[184] Because of the tradition that the twelve apostles all contributed to the declaration of faith known as the Apostles' Creed, the building exemplified the common faith and mission of the people. When the dedication

180. *The Roman Missal*, The Easter Vigil in the Holy Night 17.
181. Ordo XLI:1, p. 339.
182. PRG XXXV, p. 90.
183. PRG XXXIII:3b, p. 82.
184. PRG XXXV:1–3, p. 90–91.

exercises neared their completion, "the bishop goes back to the sacristy with the ordained ministers and puts on vestments for the other solemnities, and again the altar and the church are adorned and the candles are lighted."[185] The Mass followed the dedication in those days, so once again the rubrics linked the vesture with the lights: the clergy wore the proper vestments, and the altar candles were lighted for Mass.

In the first drafts of the preconciliar ceremony, ministers lit the candles on the walls and the altar after the anointing of the altar and *before* its incensation. Thus, whereas earlier rituals called for two separate lightings—the wall candles ablaze from the beginning, but altar candles only before the Mass—the postconciliar rite combined them. The first drafts instructed this way: "When the song [for the dedication] is over, a minister gives the bishop a small lighted candle; and two ministers bring two candles for celebrating the Sacrifice [of the Mass], which the bishop lights, and he says aloud, 'Let the light of Christ shine brightly in the Church, that all nations may attain the fullness of truth.'"[186] The addition of the two ministers was eliminated from the final rubrics, which focus on lighting the entire church from the single flame that the bishop gives the deacon. In the end, the deacon lights the candles, not the bishop.

Regarding the music for this ceremony, commentary on the first draft explained the general approach to psalms and canticles, and the challenge of the particular one assigned to the lighting of the candles:

> The psalms about Jerusalem and the house of God are sung above all (Psalms 24, 43, 87, 122, 147 . . .), but ancient anti-

---

185. PRG XXXIII:47, p. 89.
186. Schemata 370, n. 44, and Schemata 375, n. 43, p. 24.

phons edited by R. J. Hesbert may also be sung; for example, the antiphons that accompany the anointings: "Behold God's dwelling with the human race, and the Spirit of God will live with them, for the temple of God, which is you, is holy." Similarly, the canticle of Tobiah may be sung (Tobit 13), from which was taken the responsory ("The Lord has clothed you"), which cannot be sung easily at all.[187]

Indeed, the chant for the antiphon of this canticle in the sixteenth-century pontifical featured a long melisma over one of the syllables in the Latin word for "joy," which must have challenged many a schola preparing for the dedication service.[188] That antiphon slightly varied the words of the Old Vulgate's Isaiah 61:10 this way: "The Lord has clothed you in a tunic of joy and placed a crown on you. And he has adorned you with holy jewelry." It made the newly illuminated church building the object of the prophecy.

The revised liturgy has completely replaced that antiphon with two other suggestions. The verses, however, still come from chapter 13 of Tobit of the Old Vulgate, almost exactly as they appeared in the Pontifical of 1595–1596. This preserves a tradition and elicits the particular verses that interpret the lighting. In general, however, the postconciliar liturgy favors the New Vulgate of 1979. An expanded version of the same canticle of Tobit forms part of Morning Prayer for Friday of the Fourth Week of the psalter in the Liturgy of the Hours. That comes from the New Vulgate. Because these verses from the Old Vulgate are unique to this liturgy, ICEL provides its own translation of them in the ODCA.

The two antiphons proposed with the canticle from Tobit carry a missionary vision. Calabuig notes, "The first antiphon

187. Schemata 370, III:B2.
188. PR 1595–1596, p. 400, beginning with the words *"Induit te Dominus."*

is a thematic synthesis of Isaiah 60:1-3, the classic text for the solemnity of Epiphany and for missionary celebrations because of its universal perspective." Indeed, these verses are found within the first reading at the Epiphany Mass and within one possible reading for the Mass For the Evangelization of Peoples. The purpose of the light in the church is for all nations to walk by it.

The appendix of the Latin typical edition of the ODCA provides chant notation for singing these words (19), a simpler chant than the one that appeared in the preconciliar ceremony. The notes have been copied from the second antiphon at lauds of the Epiphany in the *Antiphonale Monasticum*.[189] The *Ordo Cantus Officii* has reassigned it to the third antiphon of morning prayer on the Epiphany.[190] An early English translation can be found in the Liturgy of the Hours.

The ODCA's second suggested antiphon comes from the canticle of Tobit itself, which "becomes the prophecy of the Church's perennial mission."[191] All the ends of the earth will pay homage to God. Thus, the lights do much more than decorate or provide practical illumination: They evangelize.

These decisions accomplished a few different goals. The preservation of the Canticle of Tobit as it appeared in the Old Vulgate allowed the singing of verses according to the traditional chant, whereas the changing of the historical antiphon introduced a more singable melody. Furthermore, the words proposed for the two antiphons now come directly from biblical verses. Nonetheless, the first draft permitted replacing the

---

189. *Antiphonale Monasticum Pro Diurnis Horis* (Solesmes: Desclée & Co, Tournai, 1934; S. A. La Froidfontaine, France, 1995), p. 290.

190. *Ordo cantus officii, Editio typica lltera* (Vatican City: Typis Vaticanis, 2015), p. 39.

191. Calabuig, "Commentary," p. 31.

entire Canticle of Tobit with another song "in honor of Christ, the light of the world."[192] The same permission remains in the final published order of service.

When this ritual first came under discussion in 1965, the initial preparatory group envisioned that the candles would serve a purpose beyond the day of dedication: "The style of the rubrics ought to respond to the new spirit. It is desirable here to indicate only a few examples. . . . It is appropriate that the candles beneath the crosses on the walls of the church be lighted not only on the anniversary of the church's dedication, but also on great solemnities."[193] The USCCB retained this sentiment when commenting on the rite of dedication in its guidelines for art and architecture: "The candles in these brackets are then lighted during the ritual lighting at the dedication, on anniversaries of the dedication, and on other solemn occasions."[194]

Part Four: The Liturgy of the Eucharist

As the introduction notes, "When the altar has been prepared, the Bishop celebrates the Eucharist, which is the principal part of the whole rite and also the most ancient" (ODCA II:17). The explanation cites the letter of Pope Vigilius as an early testimony to the practice, as well as a homily of St. John Chrysostom: "This altar is an object of wonder: by nature it is stone, but it is made holy after it receives the Body of Christ."[195]

192. Schemata 370, n. 45, and Schemata 375, p. 24, n. 44.
193. Schemata 67, I:7b, p. 3.
194. *Built of Living Stones*, 121.
195. ODCA II:17, citing Saint John Chrysostom, *Homilia XX in II Cor.* 3: PG 61, 540.

Significantly, the Liturgy of the Eucharist continues the same
Mass. Incorporating the rite of dedication within the Eucharist
as a single celebration marks one of the commitments of the
postconciliar reform, lending greater integrity to these liturgies.

During the years of preparation for the 1961 pontifical, the
Vatican largely reserved the celebration of any Mass to morning
hours. One member of the commission, Msgr. Enrico Dante,
objected to the possible celebration of the entire rite of dedication in an afternoon or evening for this reason. Dante served
as the Deputy in the Sacred Congregation of Rites and as the
Prefect of Papal Ceremonies. Other members of the commission in 1958, however, noted that

> the Holy Office had given a faculty to the local Ordinary to
> determine the opportunity of having Mass in the afternoon
> when such is necessary. The Commission retained the conces-
> sion for an evening Mass for the dedication rite in accordance
> with the terms established by the Holy Office: *'quando bonum
> notabilis partis fidelium id postulet'* [whenever the good
> of a notable part of the faithful may demand it] (S. Ufficio
> 404/46–236, June 11m 1957).[196]

The debate recurred in 1959. "Msgr. Dante observed that
any reference to a bishop permitting, for pastoral reasons, the
consecration of a church in the evening should be removed. A
prolonged discussion ensued. The members of the Commission were divided as to whether to permit the concession or
not."[197] In the end, the 1961 pontifical carried this note: "The
dedication of a church ordinarily happens in the morning
hours, unless the good of a notable part of the faithful sug-

196. Giampietro, *Development of the Liturgical Reform,* p. 304, n. 1053.
197. Giampietro, p. 308, n. 1108.

gests that it take place in the afternoon hours."[198] The Italian word *sera* means both "afternoon" and "evening"; both times are probably implied.

The commission's concern arose because of the existing complete separation of the Mass from the dedication. Mass began after what could have been hours of preliminary rites. Later, after the Vatican permitted evening Masses and wrapped the dedication inside the celebration of the Eucharist, these concerns retreated.

The group preparing the first draft of the ritual after the council named its incorporation into the Mass as one of its top priorities:

> *The celebration of the Mass holds the first place.* Up to now the Mass was celebrated after the dedication, often by a priest, while the bishop stood in attendance.
>
> In the new Order the lesser rites are enacted either before Mass (the entrance rite and the sprinkling of the people) or during the Liturgy of the Word and the Liturgy of the Eucharist (the deposition of the relics, anointings, lighting, incensation) or after communion (the transfer of the ciborium with the Most Blessed Sacrament). In addition, the consecratory prayer is the eucharistic prayer itself (the formulas of the proper preface and intercession).[199]

The Liturgy of the Eucharist

As the ministers prepare the altar and members of the faithful bring forward the gifts to be received by the bishop, the people sing. Recommended is this offertory chant: "Lord God, in the simplicity of my heart I have gladly offered everything; and I have looked with surpassing joy upon your people, present here.

198. PR 1961, n. 2, p. 128.
199. Schemata 370, III:A1.

God of Israel, Lord God, keep this resolve in their hearts." An alleluia is added during Easter Time (ODCA II:72 and CB 908).

The first draft had the crossbearer lead this procession of the gifts if the crucifix had not already led the entrance procession and been set in place.[200] In general, the rubrics do not call for a cross in the procession of the gifts, so this was later eliminated. The same draft proposed an alternative offertory antiphon, "I will come to the altar of God, to God, my joy and gladness," from Psalm 43:4.[201] The final version recommends only one antiphon, though it permits others.

That antiphon repeats the one from the preconciliar Missal's common for the dedication of a church. In the ODCA, the antiphon adds a second address to the "Lord God" at the end. Although those two words were absent from the preconciliar Missal, they concluded the traditional chant, still preserved in the *Graduale Romanum*. [202]

The words come from 1 Chronicles 29:17-18, part of the final prayer of David. The king had donated his wealth to the construction of the Jerusalem temple and invited others to do the same. His life came to an end just after his son Solomon was anointed king a second time and took the throne. David's final prayer acknowledged the simplicity of his heart as he offered the vastness of his wealth, and he prayed for the preservation of the people who came after him. The words make a fitting prayer of offering. The ODCA provides music for those who want to sing it as a chant.

After the bishop receives the gifts at the chair, other ministers set the altar table. Then he approaches the altar and kisses it. Mass continues in the usual way, though he does not

---

200. Schemata 370, n. 50.

201. Schemata 370, n. 51.

202. *Graduale Sacrosanctæ Romanæ Ecclesiæ de tempore et de sanctis* (Solesmes: Abbatia Sancti Petri de Solesmis, 1974), p. 401.

incense the gifts because of the elaborate incensation that has just preceded (ODCA II:73 and CB 908).

Significantly, the bishop kisses the altar. He omitted this action at his entrance to the sanctuary, when it usually takes place, because the altar had not yet been consecrated. Now he performs the displaced gesture, showing respect for this symbol of Christ and for his sacrifice. The only other object kissed in a typical celebration of Mass is the book of the gospels, another symbol of Christ. The kiss had not been included in the early drafts of the rite. To avoid any misinterpretation that the kissing of the altar signifies the beginning of the Mass, the rubric in the ODCA states clearly that the Mass "continues." The Mass does not begin at this point, as it had in the dedications of centuries past.

The bishop recites the prayer over the offerings, asking that "the gifts of your joyful Church be acceptable . . . so that your people, gathering in this holy house, may come through these mysteries to everlasting salvation" (ODCA II:74). This new prayer replaces the one from the preconciliar Missal: "O God, who are the creator of the gifts to be sanctified for you, pour out your blessing upon this house of prayer, that the help of your defense may be felt by all those calling upon your name in it." The new prayer shows the markers of postconciliar work: It captures the sense of joy in the gathering of the faithful and links the people to the place—the church within the church.

The preface is "an integral part of the Rite of the Dedication of the Church" (ODCA II:75 and CB 909). The bishop then continues with Eucharistic Prayer I or Eucharistic Prayer III. The second eucharistic prayer is for days of less solemnity, and the fourth has its own preface that cannot be replaced (GIRM 365). These restrictions were noted even in the initial drafts of the postconciliar rite.[203] The importance of the preface comes from its declaration to God, "[W]e dedicate joyfully to your

203. Schemata 370, n. 54, and Schemata 375, n. 53, p. 15.

majesty this house of prayer." Calabuig notes, "Though it is not necessary at this point in the eucharistic prayer, mention of the dedication does serve to make explicit what the eucharist effects or brings about: the dedication."[204]

The preface is the same one for the dedication of a church in the Ambrosian Rite.[205] It therefore has ideas that overlap with the prayer of dedication (II:62), which drew elements from the same preface. The Ambrosian preface, composed in Italian, was translated into Latin for the ODCA. The English translation, as is customary in the Roman Rite, is based on the Latin, rather than the Italian. For the final edition, the editors revised the Latin translation from the one proposed in the initial drafts.[206]

The preface contains multiple biblical allusions. It acknowledges God as the Creator of a world that is the temple of his glory yet allows the faithful to set aside fitting places for worship that foreshadow the heavenly Jerusalem (Heb 12:22; Rev 21:2, 10). The bishop proclaims that Christ is the temple consecrated to the Father (John 2:21 and Col 2:9) and declares that the church is the holy city built on the foundation of the apostles with Christ Jesus as the chief cornerstone (Eph 2:20). This city is built upon the members of the church, the chosen stones (1 Pet 2:5), enlivened by the Spirit and bonded in charity (Eph 3:4 and Col 3:14), a place where God will be all in all (1 Cor 15:28).

The order of service adds to each eucharistic prayer a special intercession for the occasion (ODCA II:76–77 and CB 909). These were composed for the first draft and have remained

---

204. Calabuig, "Commentary," p. 34.

205. Prefazio, Comune della dedicazione della chiesa, *Messale ambrosiano quotidiano IV, Per le celebrazioni dei santi*, p. 1182.

206. Schemata 370, n. 54, and Schemata 375, n. 53, p. 15.

unchanged.[207] The one for Eucharistic Prayer I asks the Lord to accept the oblation of those who "have offered to you this church (in honor of N.) and built it with tireless labor." It commends the actions of the people who worked hard on the construction and offer it to God. The more florid intercession for Eucharistic Prayer III may be offered by a concelebrant: "[M]ay [this church] be for your family a house of salvation and a place for the celebration of your heavenly Sacraments. Here may the Gospel of peace resound and the sacred mysteries be celebrated, so that your faithful, formed by the word of life and by divine grace on their pilgrim way through the earthly city, may merit to reach the eternal Jerusalem." It recounts the high purposes of a church for spreading the faith in this world and for guiding people toward the next.

At communion, the people are invited to sing as usual. The ODCA recommends two antiphons: "My house shall be a house of prayer, says the Lord: in that house, everyone who asks receives, and the one who seeks finds, and to the one who knocks, the door will be opened." Or "Like shoots of the olive, may the children of the Church be gathered around the table of the Lord." During Easter Time each of these ends with an alleluia (ODCA II:78).

Each is paired with Psalm 128, which enjoys frequent usage as the responsorial psalm in the Order of Celebrating Matrimony. It celebrates the joy of family life, centered on the table at home, blessed by commitment to the Lord, anticipating the eternal Jerusalem after a happy, long life. In the context of the dedication, it applies to the parish family. The second antiphon proposed for this celebration explicitly draws out this theme with a nonbiblical flourish on the psalm, directly defining the children around the table as those "of the Church."

207. Schemata 370, n. 55–56.

The first communion antiphon combines two sayings of Jesus. In one, he declares the temple a house of prayer, citing Isaiah 56:7 while cleansing the holy place of buyers and sellers (Matt 21:13, Mark 11:17, and Luke 19:45). In the other, he promises that those who ask will receive an answer to their prayers (Matt 7:8 and Luke 11:10). The new building fulfills Jesus' promise that a door will open to those who knock on it. The combination of these verses shows the sacredness and efficacy of the place and its prayers. This copies the sole antiphon for this occasion in the preconciliar Missal.

The second antiphon, the one concerning shoots of the olive, was composed for the first draft of the ritual. That draft had replaced the traditional antiphon with a different one, which it had also proposed as an alternative offertory antiphon: "I will come to the altar of God, to God my joy and gladness" (Ps 43:4). It paired this with the other verses of the same psalm. A note indicates that it was formerly used at communion on Sexagesima Sunday.[208] The ODCA did not keep it in this place. It appears in the Missal now only as an alternative entrance antiphon at the Mass for the dedication of an altar. The traditional communion antiphon was restored to the ODCA as the first option. As always, the congregation may sing other appropriate music, newly proposed or already in its repertoire.

The Inauguration of the Chapel of the Most Blessed Sacrament

If the new church incorporates a separate chapel for the tabernacle, the bishop personally inaugurates its usage. After communion, a ciborium with the remaining hosts is left on the altar as the bishop goes to the presider's chair. There, he offers the Prayer after Communion (ODCA II:79 and CB 910).

---

208. Schemata 370, n. 57, and Schemata 375, n. 56, p. 16.

This prayer leaves almost completely unchanged the first of three options for the prayer at the end of the Mass for the anniversary of the dedication of a church in the tenth-century Sacramentary of Fulda.[209] It replaces this prayer from the preconciliar Missal: "We ask you, almighty God, that you conform the ears of your fatherly love to all those repenting in this place, which we, though unworthy, have dedicated to your name."[210] The result is a prayer that honors the church's tradition while stressing the contemplative blessing that comes from sharing communion in the holy space: "instill in our minds an increase of your truth, so that we may constantly adore you in your holy temple and glory in your sight with all the Saints."

The ODCA introduced one modification to the original tenth-century prayer, changing its last phrase, "with all the holy angels," to "with all the Saints." The result draws a link between Holy Communion and the Litany of the Saints, and even more with the relics if these were placed under the altar. This modification lost, however, a strong allusion to the psalm verses upon which the prayer is based: "In the presence of the angels I praise you. I bow down toward your holy temple" (Ps 138:1-2). The original prayer thus also alluded to Matthew 18:10, where Jesus says that angels constantly behold the face of God.

To inaugurate the chapel, the bishop first goes to the altar and kneels. He incenses the Blessed Sacrament in the ciborium there. He puts on a humeral veil, picks up the ciborium, and covers it with the veil. Ministers holding the cross and candles lead the way. Priests and deacons follow them. One minister

209. *Sacramentarium Fuldense sæculi x*, Henry Bradshaw Society, Volume CI (Farnborough: Saint Michael's Abbey Press, 1977), n. 2145, p. 245.

210. *Missale Romanum, Commune Dedicationis Ecclesiæ, In ipso die Dedicationis.*

carries the bishop's pastoral staff because his hands are occupied. Two thurifers then immediately precede the bishop. His two deacons and assistants follow. All hold lighted candles and sing. Psalm 147, in which God promises to fill Jerusalem with "finest wheat," is recommended with the refrain, "O Jerusalem, glorify the Lord" (ODCA II:80 and CB 911).

At the chapel, the bishop sets the ciborium down, either inside or outside the tabernacle. Although the rubrics do not indicate it, he removes the humeral veil at that time. He incenses the Blessed Sacrament and leads all in silent prayer. Then a deacon sets the ciborium inside the tabernacle if the bishop had placed it outside, and the deacon closes the tabernacle door. A minister lights the lamp "that will burn perpetually before the Most Blessed Sacrament" (ODCA II:81 and CB 912). The burning of this lamp is in accord with a requirement in the Code of Canon Law (canon 940).

The first draft had the bishop light the candle for the chapel.[211] Because this is more the function of someone other than the presiding minister, the role appropriately changed to that of the deacon, who had lighted the other candles after the incensation of the altar.

This entire procession and inauguration is new to the postconciliar ceremony and satisfies a pastoral need. Calabuig notes, "the place of reservation is inaugurated by using it, just as the bishop had inaugurated the chair by sitting in it, and the reader had inaugurated the ambo by proclaiming from it the word of God."[212] There is no separate "blessing" of the chapel.

In the first draft, this procession was called "The Transfer of the Blessed Sacrament."[213] The introductory comments

211. Schemata 370, n. 62.
212. Calabuig, "Commentary," p. 35.
213. Schemata 370, n. 58.

explained its purpose: "To repose the Most Blessed Sacrament in the tabernacle, a procession forms in the likeness of the procession that follows the Mass of the Lord's Supper on Thursday of Holy Week."[214] Upon further reflection, however, the revisers noted the different purposes between these two similar processions. The title therefore changed from a transfer of the Blessed Sacrament to the inauguration of the chapel for its reservation. This may explain why the ODCA has the cross lead this procession, whereas it does not on Holy Thursday. The chapel becomes a way station before the cross leads the procession out of the church.

The bishop may conclude the Mass from the Blessed Sacrament chapel if the assembly can see him. If not, he returns to his chair. The procession from the chapel to the chair goes by a "shorter route," the same expression used to describe the procession that brings the ciborium from the tabernacle to the altar on Good Friday. The bishop may give the final blessing from the altar or from the chair, which is true of any Mass. Given the dedication of the altar at this Mass, an argument for blessing people from there may have more merit than usual (ODCA II:82 and CB 913).

If there is no inauguration of the Blessed Sacrament chapel, the bishop directly says the Prayer after Communion (ODCA II:83, repeating the prayer from II:79 and CB 914).

The Blessing and Dismissal

The concluding rites take place as usual. The bishop greets the people. The deacon invites them to bow down for the blessing. The bishop gives the solemn blessing specific to this occasion. The deacon dismisses the people (ODCA II:84–85 and CB 915).

---

214. Schemata 370, III:A3c.

The blessing is the same one found among the Missal's Ritual Masses for the Dedication of a Church. As with other solemn blessings, its threefold structure elicits an "Amen" from the people after each phrase.

The first drafts of this ritual gave a more expansive final rubric. Instead of simply stating, "the Deacon dismisses the people in the usual way," it proposed, "the Deacon dismisses the people in the usual way, and all leave returning thanks to God with joy."[215] Perhaps the revisers eventually discerned that the people would not read the rubric, that it was hard to command an emotion on the people, or that the Missal never commands to the people how to leave—or to leave at all. The rubrics for any Mass end with the deacon's command and the recession of the ministers. Nonetheless, the people will probably leave with joy and thanks on their own initiative.

One of the early drafts supplied an appendix for the occasion, detailing "A Celebration of Baptism Joined to the Rite of Dedication of a Church."[216] According to this proposal, if the entrance rite begins outside the doors of the church, the rite of receiving those to be baptized occurs there as well. If it begins inside, the receiving takes place after the greeting of the bishop and the presentation of the construction documents. Because of the length of the ceremony, infants to be baptized may then go to a quiet place, presumably so that they may sleep and where "other necessities" may be tended. The blessing of water in the rite of dedication suffices for providing baptismal water. The homily mentions baptism along with the dedication of the church. The patron saints of those to be baptized may be added to the litany. After the anointing of the altar, the prayer of exorcism and prebaptismal anointing take place.

215. Schemata 370, n. 64, and Schemata 375, n. 66, p. 18.
216. Schemata 375, II, p. 21.

After the altar has been prepared and the bishop has said the prayer that concludes this part of the ceremony—the prayer that was removed from this position in the final version of the ODCA—the celebration continues with the renunciation of sin and profession of faith before proceeding through the other ceremonies of baptism. After the baptism, the gifts of bread and wine for the celebration of the Lord's Supper are brought forward, and Mass continues as usual. This proposed appendix gave a fuller description for incorporating baptism into Mass than the Order of Baptism of Children itself had offered in its first edition.

Even though this description showed a helpful way to intertwine the two ceremonies, it was removed from the final version of the ODCA. It is not clear why the appendix first appeared or why it was removed. Perhaps it was added as a pastoral outreach for growing families in the parish community or to show the similarity of symbols in the two rites of baptism and dedication. Perhaps it was removed to discourage the blending of two occasions that each deserve independent attention or to avoid amplifying the length of the dedication ceremony that the revisers had worked so hard to improve through abbreviation.

The ceremony of dedication that remains stands as a tribute to the vibrant liturgical work at the time of the Second Vatican Council. It affirms the holiness of the people of God. It connects the bishop to the parishes of his diocese. It builds on a colorful history of dedication ceremonies. It rearranges the parts of the service to clarify their meaning. It provides a memorable event in the history of a parish that will dedicate a building, its altar, and its people to God.

CHAPTER III

The Order of the Dedication of a Church in Which Sacred Celebrations Are Already Regularly Taking Place

Some churches and altars have been in use for some time, even though they were never formally dedicated. This has been a circumstance throughout the history of Christianity. To cite one extraordinary example, Pope Alexander III laid the cornerstone for the cathedral of Notre Dame in Paris in March or April of 1163; the altar was consecrated on May 19, 1182; and the church was dedicated on May 13, 1864—seven centuries later.[1]

Still, the bishops of the United States cautioned, "To celebrate the rite after the altar has been in use is anti-climactic and can reduce the rite to empty symbolism. Use of a temporary altar in the period before the dedication is a viable alternative that can help to heighten anticipation of the day of dedication when the new altar will receive the ritual initiation that solemnly prepares it for the celebration of the central mystery of our faith."[2]

1. Evenou, "Le nouveau rituel," p. 90.
2. *Built of Living Stones*, 119.

The Introduction to this section explains that it may be used only if the altar has never been dedicated either. The dedication of a church requires also the dedication of its altar. This ritual takes place when a recently constructed building has been used for Mass before its dedication or when "something new or greatly changed" has happened to the physical building or to its purpose (ODCA III:1 and CB 916). For example, a complete restoration of an existing church may call for this ceremony. Or a building formerly blessed as a chapel or oratory with the order of service in Chapter V of the ODCA is now becoming a parish church, requiring the dedication in Chapter III.

This occasion simplifies the ceremonies of Chapter II. The rite of opening the doors is omitted unless the church that was formerly in use has been closed for a long period of time. The rite of handing over the church to the bishop is retained only if it seems appropriate. The sprinkling of the walls with holy water is omitted because it is "purificatory by its very nature," and the previous celebrations of the Eucharist have already purified them. Those parts relating to the first proclamation of the Word of God are omitted, including the otherwise required first reading from Nehemiah (ODCA III:2 and CB 917).

Part One: The Introductory Rites

The Entrance

The entrance resembles the third form in the previous chapter: The vested ministers move from the sacristy through the nave to the sanctuary. If relics are to be placed in the altar, these are brought from the sanctuary or from the chapel where they were venerated overnight, or they stand already in the sanctuary in the place prepared for them before Mass. The music recommended for the procession is the same one in ODCA II:45, "God is in his holy place, God who unites those who dwell in his house; he himself gives might and strength to his people" with Psalm 122 (ODCA III:1–5). Alternatively, the antiphon from ODCA II:32 may be used, "Let us go rejoicing to the house of the Lord."

As the ministers take their places, the bishop goes to his chair without kissing the altar, as in ODCA II:35, 42, and 46. He greets the people with any liturgical greeting, but the one recommended in Chapter II is also suggested here: "May grace and peace be with you all in the holy Church of God." If it seems appropriate, the bishop may receive the construction documents, as in the previous chapter—or this may be omitted (ODCA III:6–7).

The Blessing and Sprinkling of Water
The bishop blesses and sprinkles water on the people "as a sign of repentance and as a remembrance of Baptism." He does not sprinkle the walls of the church because they have already been in use. He may, however, sprinkle the altar if it is "completely new." This probably accounts for the possibility that the altar has been previously blessed according to the ceremony in Chapter VI; such an altar will be anointed with chrism in this ritual but not sprinkled in purification because of its prior use.

A comparison with the prayer in ODCA II:48 shows that all references to sprinkling the walls have been moved, along with the declaration that by this action, the walls and altar "will be purified." During the sprinkling, the same antiphons from the full order of dedication are suggested again. To conclude the rite, the bishop prays that God will "cleanse us who are the temple where he dwells," as he does in the previous chapter, but he omits what he says at the dedication of a previously unused church, that God may "dwell in this house of prayer" (II:49). God has already dwelled among the people at the Eucharist in this place (ODCA III:8–10).

The Hymn and the Collect

As in Chapter II:51–52, the assembly sings the Gloria, and the bishop offers the collect. This order of service makes no change to that prayer (ODCA III:11–12).

Part Two: The Liturgy of the Word

All are seated to hear the readings. The ceremonies that accompanied the first use of the ambo in Chapter II are omitted because the Word of God has been proclaimed in this building. Any of the readings from the lectionary's selections from the Rite of Dedication of a Church may be proclaimed. A commentary on these can be found in the treatment of ODCA II:54b above.

The rubric for the Liturgy of the Word directs the reader to the Lectionary for Mass 816 to find a selection of readings (ODCA III:13). That section offers only one option for the first reading: Nehemiah 8:2-4a, 5-6, 8-10, and one option for the responsorial psalm: Psalm 19:8-9, 10, 15, together with a refrain from John 6:63c. The Introduction, however, excludes both of these from consideration, saying that, instead of them, "another suitable reading is chosen" (III:2d). It offers no further advice.

One solution is to choose a first reading from the Dedication of an Altar in Lectionary for Mass 817, which offers three possibilities:

Genesis 28:11-18 is the account of Jacob pouring oil onto a stone altar that he erected after his vision of angels on a ladder to and from heaven. It shows the antiquity of anointing an altar as a place of encounter with God.

Joshua 8:30-35 recounts how Joshua built an altar to the Lord. This is one of several places in the Old Testament where religious leaders identified holy places with an altar of sacrifice.

1 Maccabees 4:52-59 tells of the dedication of an altar that brought joy to the people after recapturing their stolen temple.

Although the dedication ceremony underway probably responds to a different pastoral need, it somewhat parallels this account of restoring a previously used holy space.

If the dedication takes place during Easter Time, the lectionary offers two different options for the first reading (818):

Acts of the Apostles 2:42-47 tells of the idyllic beginnings of community life among the first Christians, who broke bread and offered prayers together. They performed these actions in their homes, probably using the family table as the altar of the Eucharist. The recollection of those days may help the present community interpret their eucharistic gathering in the light of a large family meal.

Revelation 8:3-4 relates John's vision of an angel with a golden censer, who offered incense and prayers on the golden altar that was God's throne. This passage contains the recommended antiphons for the incensation of a newly dedicated altar.

From the same section on dedicating an altar, Lectionary 819 offers five possibilities for the responsorial psalm.

Psalm 84:3-4, 5 and 10, 11 comes from a pilgrimage song encountered elsewhere in the order of dedication, singing of the beauty of God's dwelling place. As a refrain all may sing either verse 2 of the psalm ("How lovely is your dwelling place, Lord, mighty God!") or a phrase from Revelation 21:3b ("Here God lives among his people" or "God who is with them will be their God.") In such refrains, the community sings of the beauty and glory of God in the church now being dedicated.

Psalm 95:1-2, 3-5, 6-7 extends an invitation to worship God, complete with the refrain "Let us come before the Lord and praise him." At the dedication ceremony, these words may summon the community to renew the purpose of their prayer.

Psalm 118:15-16, 19-20, 22-23, 27 is another passage found elsewhere in the ceremonies of dedication. It calls for an opening of gates and acclaims a stone rejected by builders that has become the cornerstone. It bears the refrain, "Give thanks, for the Lord is good; his love is everlasting." Even though the gates of this church have already been opened, the dedication of the altar as a symbol of Christ justifies the recollection of the psalm verse that the New Testament interprets as a prophecy for the coming of Christ, the once-rejected and now central stone.

Psalm 119:125, 130, 133, 135, 144 comes from the longest psalm of the Bible, each verse a meditation on the beauty of God's law. The refrain, "Your word, O Lord, is a lamp for my feet," highlights better the function of the ambo. This same psalm appears in the Book of Blessings as one recommended for inaugurating a new presidential chair (1167) or a new lectern (1184). It could help the community meditate on one purpose of the liturgy, even though its ambo has already been in use.

Psalm 122:1-2, 3-4 and 8-9 comes from a beloved pilgrimage song of entering the holy city of Jerusalem. In context, it would serve less as a psalm of first entry into the holy space and more as a joyful song of return to a beloved place, now receiving its awaited dedication.

For the proclamation of the gospel, neither candles nor incense accompany the procession (ODCA III:14), as in the full rite of dedication (II:54b). The solemn incensation and lighting of candles for the altar and the church follow later.

As expected, the bishop preaches the homily, and all profess the Creed. The universal prayer is omitted because this ceremony includes the Litany of the Saints (ODCA III:15–16).

Part Three: The Prayer of Dedication and the Anointings

The entire third part of the liturgy is identical to the full rite for the dedication of a new church and altar. The Litany of Supplication, the optional Deposition of Relics, The Prayer of Dedication, The Anointing of the Altar and the Walls of the

Church, The Incensation of the Altar and the Church, and The Lighting of the Altar and the Church (ODCA III:17–31) repeat all the information detailed earlier (II:57–71).

The second presentation of the same material makes the liturgical book easier to use during the ceremony. The bishop and ministers responsible for the liturgy need not flip pages back and forth, risking the loss of one's place and the reading of the wrong prayers in the middle of a complicated liturgy.

Part Four: The Liturgy of the Eucharist

The fourth part of the liturgy (ODCA III:32–40) repeats the essential elements of the previous chapter (II:72–85) with only a few differences. The preface for the dedication of a new church is replaced with another one for a church already in use, and the special intercessions that are inserted into Eucharistic Prayer I or III for the dedication of a new church do not take place in this instance. If the Blessed Sacrament chapel is to be inaugurated, the ritual book refers the ministers back to the previous chapter—the only place in this chapter where the complete texts do not reappear.

The preface is the one assigned to the Mass on the anniversary of the dedication of a church, the first of the presidential prayers grouped under the Commons in the Missal. It was newly composed for the postconciliar Missal, and it mentions the people "on pilgrimage," an image popular with the Second Vatican Council. "Pilgrim Church" is the heading of chapter VII of *Lumen Gentium*, the council's Dogmatic Constitution on the Church.

Blending the themes of the church as building and as people, this preface alludes to several biblical passages: "the temple that we are" recalls 1 Corinthians 3:17 and 6:19, as well as 2 Corinthians 6:16; "to grow ever more and more as the Lord's own

Body" recalls Ephesians 4:15-16; and "the vision of peace, the heavenly city of Jerusalem" recalls Hebrews 12:22, Revelation 3:12, and Revelation 21:2-3, 10.[3]

The special intercessions inserted into the eucharistic prayers are not repeated in the case of a church already in use because they imply that this is the first celebration of the Eucharist in a new space. The first speaks of the servants who "have offered to you this church (in honor of N.) and build it with tireless labor" (II:76), and the other prays that the building may be "a house of salvation and a place for the celebration of your heavenly Sacraments." The same intercession speaks of some future events: "Here may the Gospel of peace resound," for example. This has already been happening.

The ceremony for dedicating a church already in use borrows heavily from the ceremony for a church enjoying its first usage, making some sensible adjustments to preserve the integrity of the words and actions of the Mass.

3. Anthony Ward and Cuthbert Johnson, *The Prefaces of the Roman Missal: A Source Compendium with Concordance and Indices*, Congregatio for *Divine Worship* (Rome: C.L.V.—Editioni Liturgiche, 1989), pp. 353–54.

The Order of the Dedication of an Altar

The fourth chapter addresses the situation where a new altar has been installed in a previously dedicated church. It is useful, for example, in churches built before the council whose members have installed a freestanding altar or in churches replacing an older altar proven inadequate because of size, material, deterioration, or some other concern.

Again, the circumstance is not new. The thirteenth-century Pontifical of Durandus detailed the ceremony as well. "When only the altar and not the church is consecrated, which may take place on any day, though it more appropriately takes place on Sundays and feast days, the things necessary for it are to be prepared."[1] As with the combined ceremony for the dedication of the church and altar, the bishop of previous centuries celebrated this liturgy apart from Mass. Upon completing the complex ceremonies consecrating the altar, "the bishop goes into the sacristy and prepares himself for Mass if he wishes."[2] Often, the bishop let a priest celebrate the Mass, partly because

1. Durand II III:1, p. 478.
2. Durand II III:81, p. 496.

the parts restricted to the bishop had come to an end and partly
because the preceding taxing ceremonies argued in favor of
giving the bishop a rest.

That has changed. Now the dedication of an altar takes place
within the celebration of the Eucharist, and the bishop presides
for it all (ODCA IV:22). Bugnini summarized the work of the
committee: "The characteristic moments in this dedication
(which is performed, as always, during Mass) are: sprinkling
of the faithful and the altar after the greeting and opening
address; then, after the homily, the Litany of the Saints, deposition of relics, prayer of dedication, anointing, lighting of
incense, lighting of the altar. This Mass likewise has its proper
texts."[3]

Mass is not to be celebrated on the new altar until after its
dedication (ODCA IV:13). The selected day should favor the
gathering of "as many of the faithful as possible," especially
a Sunday. However, certain days are excluded: the Paschal
Triduum, Ash Wednesday, weekdays of Holy Week, and All
Souls' Day (ODCA IV:14 and CB 922 and 924). If the dedication takes place on Christmas, Epiphany, Ascension, Pentecost, or on a Sunday of Advent, Lent, or Easter Time, the
bishop offers the presidential prayers of that Mass, except for
the Prayer over the Offerings and Preface, which are always part
of this ceremony (ODCA IV:15 and CB 925). Concelebration,
especially by priests associated with the church, is encouraged
(ODCA IV:16 and CB 926).

The Introduction to this order of service offers an excellent
meditation on the purpose and symbolism of the altar: a sign
of Christians, the table of sacrifice and of the paschal banquet,
a sign of Christ, and the honor of the martyrs (ODCA V:1–5).

3. Bugnini, *Reform of the Liturgy*, pp. 796–97.

This section provides useful catechesis for anyone seeking insight into the meaning of the altar in Catholic spirituality.

A fixed altar is desirable for every church, though movable ones are acceptable in other places (GIRM 298). New churches are to have only one altar, "so that in the one assembly of the faithful the one altar may be a sign of our one Savior Jesus Christ and the one Eucharist of the Church" (ODCA IV 6–7 and CB 919). This marks a departure from previous constructions that favored multiple fixed altars in the same church. Another altar may be erected in a chapel for the Blessed Sacrament, for the celebration of daily Mass, but "the erection of several altars in a church merely for the sake of adornment must be entirely avoided" (IV:7).

The same Introduction makes other points. Citing GIRM 299, it continues, "The altar should be built separate from the wall, in such a way that the Priest can easily walk around it and celebrate Mass facing the people" (ODCA IV:8). Traditionally, the altar is made of stone, but other materials may be used (IV:9). Even if relics are kept beneath the altar or images of saints stand nearby, the altar is dedicated to God, not to any saint (IV:10–11).

Part One: The Introductory Rites

The first part of the liturgy opens as any Mass does; however, the sprinkling of blessed water replaces the penitential act, even if the ceremony does not take place on a Sunday (ODCA IV:17).

The vested ministers enter the church following the processional cross. If there are relics to be placed beneath the altar, these are either carried in procession or set in a dignified place beforehand (ODCA IV:31–32 and CB 933–934). The list of ministers does not include the one carrying incense because its use is deferred from the opening rite of this liturgy. The first

draft of this ceremony in January of 1972 made more explicit
the omission of incense at the entrance.[4]

Psalm 43 is recommended for the entrance procession
(ODCA IV:33). In the ceremonies that involve the dedication
of a church, the pilgrimage-inspired Psalm 122 is suggested.
Here, however, the church has already been in use. Two refrains are recommended. The first is Psalm 84:10, "Turn your
eyes, O God, our shield, and look on the face of your Anointed
one: one day within your courts is better than a thousand elsewhere." The second is verse 4 of Psalm 43 itself: "I will come
to the altar of God, the God who restores the joy of my youth."
The first draws a prophetic comparison between the anointed
king of the psalm and the altar, which represents Christ. The
second focuses the procession on its ultimate destiny, the central place of the sanctuary: the altar (ODCA IV:33 and CB 935).
The preconciliar ceremony used Psalm 43 with this second
refrain.[5] The first draft proposed either the antiphon from
Psalm 84 alone or the antiphon from Psalm 43 with some
verses of that psalm.[6] Now Psalm 43 is recommended with
either antiphon.

The Roman Gradual offers two different recommendations
for the Entrance at this ceremony. It pairs Isaiah 59:21 and
56:7. God promises that his words will remain forever and that
acceptable sacrifices will be offered on the altar. It also offers an
expanded set of verses from Psalm 84 (10 and 11, then 2 and 3).

As the bishop goes to his chair, he does not kiss the altar
because it has not yet been consecrated. He may use any li-

4. Sacra Congregatio pro Cultu Divino, Coetus a Studiis XXI bis, *Ordo
dedicationis altaris*, 6 January 1972, Schemata 378, De Pont. n. 27, De dec.
alt. 2, n. 4, p. 11.

5. PR 1595–1596, pp. 409–10, and PR 1961, pp. 165–66.

6. Schemata 378, n. 3, p. 10.

turgical greeting of the people, but recommended is the one from the dedication of the church (ODCA II:30, for example, and III:6): "May grace and peace be with you all in the holy Church of God" (ODCA IV:34 and CB 936).

The bishop blesses water and sprinkles it first upon the people, then upon the altar. The ceremony is a sign of repentance and remembrance of the people's baptism and of "purifying the altar." All sing during the sprinkling. The bishop concludes with a prayer (ODCA IV:35–37 and CB 937–939).

The bishop's introduction to the blessing of water is longer than its equivalent in ODCA II:48 because he incorporates elements into it from the introduction to the entire liturgy of the blessing of a church (II:30). In this, his first opportunity to explain the ceremonies, he gives more detail. Any references to blessing the church have been removed, and the introduction focuses on dedicating a new altar, which will be accomplished "by celebrating the Lord's Sacrifice" (IV:35). The first draft kept these introductions separate,[7] but they have been combined into an integrated whole.

The antiphons recommended for singing at the sprinkling are the same from the dedication of a church (II:49). The second was slightly briefer in the first draft.[8]

The concluding prayer to the sprinkling differs from its equivalent in the dedication of a church, which asks God to "dwell in this house of prayer" and cleanse those "who are the temple where he dwells" (II:50). The bishop replaces that with the more fitting prayer: "May God the Father of mercies, to whom we dedicate this new altar on earth, grant us remission of sins and allow us to offer the sacrifice of praise for all

7. Schemata 378, n. 5–6, p. 11.
8. Schemata 378, n. 7, p. 12.

eternity at his altar on high" (IV:37). The first draft put no prayer here at all.[9]

All sing the Gloria, and the bishop leads the collect for the Mass (ODCA IV:38–39 and CB 939). The collect is new to this ritual. Its acclamation of Christ "lifted high on the altar of the Cross" is probably an allusion to Jesus' promise that, when lifted high, he would draw all to himself (John 12:32). The point of this prayer is to ask God "to fill [the] Church . . . with heavenly grace as she dedicates . . . this altar." The bishop is praying for the people who will celebrate the Eucharist here.

Part Two: The Liturgy of the Word

During the second part of the liturgy, the readings are proclaimed as usual. The bishop preaches the homily, and all recite the Creed. The universal prayer is omitted because of the upcoming Litany of the Saints (ODCA IV:18–19 and 40–42, and CB 940–942). The first draft had explicitly omitted the Creed,[10] but it has been restored. The same draft explained a little of the purpose of the bishop's homily: "he explains the biblical readings and the meaning of the rite by which the altar is dedicated to God and the table is prepared for the banquet of the holy people."[11]

On certain occasions, the readings are drawn from the Mass for the day. If the dedication of the altar takes place on Christmas, Epiphany, Ascension, Pentecost, or any Sunday of Advent, Lent, or Easter, then the readings already assigned to that day are proclaimed. Otherwise, they may come from the lectionary's options for the Mass for the Dedication of an Altar

9. Schemata 378, n. 8, p. 12.
10. Schemata 378, n. 10b, p. 13.
11. Schemata 378, n. 11, p. 13.

(817–822). Commentary on the first readings and responsorials may be found above in the treatment of Part Two from Chapter III, The Order of the Dedication of a Church in Which Sacred Celebrations Are Already Regularly Taking Place.

For the second reading, the lectionary offers two options from the New Testament (820):

In 1 Corinthians 10:16-21, St. Paul declares that the wine and bread blessed and broken admit the community into a participation in the Blood and Body of Christ. Those who eat such sacrifices, Paul says, participate at the altar. Because this letter was composed even before the gospels, it provides some of the earliest testimony of Christian usage of an altar.

The letter to the Hebrews (13:8-15) distinguishes the sacrifice at the altar of the temple and the sacrifice of praise offered by the people who confess the name of Jesus. This passage places the Christian usage of an altar within its historical context, reaching all the way back to the sacrifices in the temple of Solomon.

The short texts that supply the alleluia verse and verse before the gospel come from various biblical sources (821):

In Ezekiel 37:27, God proclaims that his dwelling is with the people who are his own. This foreshadows the presence of God in the people who worship in the dedicated churches of the new covenant.

The second option is based on a line from the conversation between Jesus and the Samaritan woman at the well (John 4:23, 24). The Father seeks those who worship him in Spirit and in truth. Right worship requires a proper intention, not just a dedicated altar. The people are experiencing an impressive ceremony focusing on a piece of furniture, but they hear frequent reminders to make their own prayer sincere.

Hebrews 13:8 comes from one of the options for the second reading, and it proclaims that Jesus Christ is the same yesterday, today, and forever. As the altar represents Christ, it remains forever a symbol of him in the midst of the people.

Finally, the lectionary offers three options for the gospel at the Mass for the dedication of an altar (822):

In Matthew 5:23-24, Jesus tells the disciples not to offer a gift at the altar without first reconciling with their brothers and sisters. Having a dedicated altar is not enough: God accepts offerings that come from people of virtue.

John 4:19-24 presents a larger section of Jesus' full encounter with the woman of Samaria at the well. When the conversation turns to the appropriate place for worship, Jesus says that all must worship in Spirit and in truth. Ultimately, that includes this community witnessing the dedication of its new altar.

In John 12:31-36a, Jesus, facing his impending execution, offers a message of hope: He will draw all people to himself when he is lifted up from the earth. Each celebration of the Eucharist participates in the mystery of the cross of Christ the redeemer.

Part Three: The Prayer of Dedication and the Anointings

The introductory material for this section (ODCA IV:20–22) repeats most of the equivalent section from the chapter on the dedication of a church (II:14–16). It eliminates references to the dedicating, incensing, and lighting of the walls of the church because these do not take place. Instead, it focuses on ceremonies pertaining to the altar. It also eliminates the explanation that the sacrifices of the members are drawn into the sacrifice of Christ the Head. The church building more clearly symbolizes the community, whereas the altar represents Christ. The building has already been dedicated, so this section does not stress this interplay of sacrifices.

The Litany of Supplication

The ceremony begins with the Litany of Supplication: the invitation from the bishop, the chanting of the names of the saints, and the bishop's closing prayer (ODCA IV:43–46 and CB 943). This is almost identical to the litany in the dedication of a church (ODCA II:57–61). The bishop's invitation, however, is quite different. When dedicating a church, he states that God "makes the hearts of the faithful into spiritual temples for himself," but when dedicating an altar in a church that already is forming the community as spiritual temples, his introduction focuses on the saints, one of whom may have relics to be placed under the altar, and all of whom "are joined as sharers in [Christ's] suffering and companions at his table."

In the litany, the only change is one to be expected, occurring in the petitions at the end. Instead of asking God to consecrate "this church," the cantors ask God to consecrate "this altar."

The bishop's concluding prayer changes from one about the dedicated building and "house of salvation and grace" to one about the altar, "a place where the great mysteries of salvation are accomplished and where your people offer you gifts, make known their desires, pour out their prayers, and bring forth every sentiment of worship and devotion."

The first draft of this ritual made a reference to 1 Timothy 2:5 that does not appear in the final version. Before the community was to invoke all the saints, the bishop invited the prayers of the community to ascend "through Jesus Christ, the only mediator." In light of that passage, the Second Vatican Council's Constitution on the Church relativized the intercession of the saints: they intercede with the Father through the one mediator between God and humanity, Jesus Christ (*Lumen Gentium* 49).[12] The typical edition removed the reference to

---

12. Chengalikavil, "Dedicazione della chiesa," p. 82.

Christ as the only mediator. Perhaps the revisers felt that its inclusion would have made people wonder why they should then call upon a list of saints, and its omission clears the way for following this tradition.

ICEL's original translation of a phrase in the concluding prayer would have harmonized with 1 Timothy 2:5. Instead of "through the intercession of the Blessed Virgin Mary and all the Saints," the English language draft proposed "at the intercession of the Blessed Virgin Mary and all the Saints." This distinction would have shown that Christ remains the only mediator, whereas the saints accompany the community in their petition. The Vatican, however, prefers the familiar English translation "through the intercession of." The same preference is evident throughout the Roman Missal.

The Deposition of the Relics

If there are relics of a saint, these may be set under the altar after the litany (ODCA IV:47 and CB 944). The explanation for this ceremony is identical to the one in the dedication of a church, including the recommended antiphons and psalm (ODCA II:61).

As in the dedication of a church, documents pertaining to the altar may be sealed inside it with the relics: "It is fitting to observe the practice of enclosing a parchment in the reliquary on which is recorded the day, the month, and the year of the dedication of the altar, the name of the Bishop who celebrated the rite, the Title of the church, and the names of the Martyrs of Saints whose relics are to be deposited under the altar" (IV:30). This is almost identical to the permission given in ODCA II:25, except for those matters pertaining to the details of dedicating the church. In English as in Latin, the two paragraphs in IV:30 reverse the order of the parallel paragraphs in II:25. Perhaps this was to highlight the documents placed in the altar because the church has already been dedicated.

The Prayer of Dedication

The bishop offers the lengthy prayer of dedication, the heart of this ceremony in which the altar is set aside for worship to God (ODCA IV:48 and CB 945). This marks a significant change from the first draft of this liturgy, which had no prayer of dedication over the altar, while retaining the other symbols: anointing, incensation, and lighting.[13] This had been true of the 1961 pontifical as well.[14] The celebration of the Eucharist itself was to consecrate the altar. The introduction to the draft explained it this way:

> The celebration of the Eucharist is the primary and necessary element (*res*) for dedicating an altar. The Eucharist, however, is not celebrated principally that the altar coming in contact with Holy Things may become holy, but that the Christian community fully enacting the Memorial of the Lord may participate in the paschal mystery: for an altar is erected for that purpose.
>
> In the rite of the dedication of an altar, the proper Preface is the one most powerful prayer of all and therefore may never be omitted; therefore, Eucharistic Prayer IV may not be used.[15]

This thinking obviously changed, and a prayer of dedication of the altar proper has been added to the liturgy. The preconciliar rite's "preface" for the dedication of an altar served as an inspiration, though the result is essentially a new prayer. The previous rite had the bishop offer two separate prefaces, one to dedicate the church and the other to dedicate the altar. The preconciliar preface for the altar listed a series of sacrificial

13. Schemata 378, n. 17, p. 16.
14. PR 1961, p. 172.
15. Schemata 378, III:21, p. 8.

prototypes from the Old Testament: the offerings of Abel, Abraham, Melchizedek, Isaac, Jacob, and Moses.[16]

The new prayer glorifies the Lord who decreed that altars reach their fulfillment in Christ. It recalls the altars of Noah (Gen 8:20-21), Abraham (Gen 22:9-10 and Rom 4:9, 11), and Moses (Exod 24:6).

In the case of Moses, the previous prayer had conflated two passages from Exodus. In the first (Exod 24:6), Moses, having received the commandments, set up twelve pillars that the previous prayer interpreted as a foreshadowing of the apostles. In the second passage (Exod 29:36-37), the Lord commanded Moses to purify an altar with sin offerings spread over seven days. This made it most holy, the holy of holies, so that whatever touched it would also become holy. The preconciliar prayer of dedication interpreted the Christian altar as one that purified people from sin through the most sacred point of contact where bread and wine would become the Body and Blood of Christ.

The new prayer, however, abandoned the images of the apostles, purification, and the holiness of things that touch the altar in favor of a reference to the sprinkling of an animal's blood that prefigures the blood of Christ poured out on the altar of the cross. The new prayer does, however, change the animal from the cattle mentioned in Exodus 24 to the lamb whose blood was sprinkled on doorposts at Israel's flight from Egypt (Exod 12:21-22).

The new prayer of dedication thus highlights the paschal mystery of Christ, who handed himself over on the cross as a pure oblation. The bishop prays that the Lord will "pour forth from heaven your sanctifying power upon this altar, built in the house of the Church, that it may be an altar dedicated for

16. PR 1595-1596, pp. 430-35.

all time by the sacrifice of Christ, and stand as the Lord's table where your people are refreshed by the divine banquet." The altar symbolizes the pierced side of Christ, from which flowed blood and water, establishing the sacraments of the church (John 19:34). Whereas the prayer of dedication of a church explores the future usages of the building, this prayer celebrates the purposes of the altar: "a festive table" where Christians "gain new strength of spirit for new paths ahead," "the place of intimate communion with you and a place of peace," "the source of the Church's unity," and "the center of our praise and thanksgiving."

The prayer imagines that the altar is made from stone, "cut and shaped," or more literally, "cut and polished." It permits an alternative version, however, when the altar is made of another material.

The prayer contrasts with its predecessor, which made petitions for innocence, the destruction of pride, the slaughter of wrath, the removal of passions, and the provision of a sacrificial place for the chaste and innocent.[17] The new listing of the altar's purposes draws together many themes of the council: the spirit of "joy," the taking of "new paths ahead," "peace," the coming of "the Spirit," "the Church's unity," "praise and thanksgiving," and the hopes of this community to come "jubilant to eternal dwellings."

The Anointing of the Altar

The bishop may remove his chasuble or leave it on. He binds the gremial over his vestments and approaches the altar with the deacon, who carries the chrism. The bishop offers a prayer and then pours the chrism on the middle and four corners of the altar. He may anoint the entire mensa. Meanwhile, the

17. PR 1595–1596, p. 435.

people sing; Psalms 45 and 118 are recommended with anti-phons. Afterwards, ministers assist the bishop as he washes his hands (ODCA IV:49–52 and CB 946).

The bishop's prayer is a version of the one before the anointing during the dedication of a church (ODCA II:64). In that one, he prays that "this altar and this house . . . may express the mystery of Christ and the Church." Here he prays that "this altar . . . may express the mystery of Christ, who offered himself to the Father for the life of the world." It concentrates squarely on the altar as a symbol of Christ and his cross. This prayer has not changed since the first postconciliar draft of this ceremony.[18]

The recommended psalms and antiphons are particular to this occasion. The parallel anointing in the dedication of the church employed words that pertained to the building. Here, they align with anointing an altar. The rubrics recommend this refrain paired with Psalm 45: "God, your God, has anointed you, above your companions with the oil of gladness." That comes from verse 8 of the same psalm, which Hebrews 1:9 cites as a prophecy for Christ. Psalm 118, recommended for Easter Time, is paired with the antiphon, "The stone which the builders rejected has become the cornerstone, alleluia," which comes from verse 22 of the same psalm. Both of these were proposed even in the first draft of the postconciliar ceremony.[19] They demonstrate the church's frequent application of psalm verses to show their fulfillment in Christ.

The Incensation of the Altar

Ministers place a brazier for burning incense on top of the altar or a heap of incense mixed with wax tapers. The bishop ignites the incense and offers a prayer. He adds grains to a thurible and

---

18. Schemata 378, n. 18, p. 16.
19. Schemata 378, n. 19, p. 17.

incenses the altar. A minister incenses first the bishop and then the people, all of whom may sing. Psalm 138 is recommended, especially for its verses, "In the presence of the angels I praise you. I bow down toward your holy temple" (ODCA IV:53 and CB 947). This creates a visual and textual image of the angel with the golden censer before the altar of God (Rev 8:3-4).

This ceremony replicates the one for the incensation of a church and an altar, except for the incensation of the walls (ODCA II:66–68). The antiphons from that ritual, which already concern incense at the altar, remain unchanged.

The bishop's prayer also repeats the one from the dedication of the church in Chapter II. He alludes to Psalm 141:2, hoping that the prayers will rise like incense, and he notes that "this house is filled with a pleasing fragrance" because the effect of the incense is the same: It is smelled throughout the building, not just at the altar. His petition, then, is likewise the same: "let your Church be fragrant with the aroma of Christ." However, the first draft for this ceremony proposed a different prayer: "Let our prayer rise, O Lord, like incense in your sight; and as this altar is fragrant with a pleasing aroma, so may the children of the Church spread the good fragrance of Christ."[20] It thus noted the fragrance of the altar, not of the church, and made the spread of the fragrance an evangelical imperative, not a merely olfactory affair. The same draft had the bishop incense the altar and the cross; now he incenses just the altar. The incensation of the cross that usually takes place during the preparation of the gifts will be omitted.

In the first draft, the lighting of the candles preceded the anointing of the altar.[21] The sequence was reversed before the publication of the typical edition. Apparently, the preferred

20. Schemata 378, n. 21, p. 19.
21. Schemata 378, n. 20, p. 18.

sequence keeps the anointing closer to the dedication prayer, the incensing closer to the anointing, while putting the lighting later to celebrate the unity of those gathered at the altar.

The Covering and the Lighting of the Altar

Ministers wipe the altar with cloths and may cover it with non-porous linen to protect the altar cloth from excessive contact with chrism. They set the altar cloth in place and may decorate the altar with flowers and candles, and, if necessary, the altar cross (ODCA IV:54 and CB 948). This repeats the instructions from the order of dedication of a church (ODCA II:69).

The bishop gives a taper to the deacon, offers a prayer, and the deacon lights the altar candles. Other candles and even electrical lights around the altar are lit as all sing. The actions repeat those from the dedication of a church (II:70–71), except that the candles on the walls of the church are not lighted at this time, and the antiphon is different (IV:55–56 and CB 949–950). If the church has festive candles on the walls from its day of dedication, these would appropriately have been lighted before the beginning of this Mass. This ceremony pertains to the lighting of the altar candles.

The bishop's prayer, therefore, is slightly adjusted. When dedicating the church, he prays that the light of Christ may shine in the Church and "that all nations may attain the fullness of truth." But when about to have the altar candles lighted, he prays that the light of Christ may "shine upon the table of this altar" and that "those who share the Lord's Supper [may] shine with his light." Thus, the lighting has more to do with the gathered church at the altar than with the evangelical church represented by the building.

The draft already contained these words of the bishop, and it had one extra note in the rubrics. Instead of "Then the festive lighting takes place," the original draft read, "Then, as a sign of joy, the festive lighting of the altar and the church takes place."[22] Perhaps "a sign of joy" is to be understood with the word "festive." The command to light the entire church, not just the altar, has been wisely removed.

The recommended antiphon is "With you, O Lord, is the fountain of life, and in your light we see light" (Ps 36:9). The original draft suggested "The Lord is my light and my salvation" (Ps 27:1), along with the rest of the same psalm. The new antiphon sets aside that one, which could have focused overmuch on personal faith. Instead, it alludes to the fruits of the Eucharist at this altar, "the fountain of life." It also acclaims that all see light in the light of Christ by the candles of this altar.

The first draft for this entire part of the liturgy concluded with a prayer that has been removed: "O God, the worship of whom is our nourishment, pour out your abundant grace upon this table, and plant more deeply into your faithful people the mystery of redemption that will befit them, and refresh them with sacramental sustenance. Through Christ our Lord."[23] This was probably composed as a parallel to the prayer originally envisioned at this point in the dedication of a church—the prayer that became the collect for that celebration. In both cases, any prayer at this point probably seemed superfluous, given the ceremonies the preceded and the Liturgy of the Eucharist to come.

Part Four: The Liturgy of the Eucharist

The last part of the Mass continues as usual, though with specially assigned texts (ODCA IV:57–64 and CB 951–953). An antiphon at the offertory is recommended, as is music at communion. The

---

22. Schemata 378, n. 20, p. 18.
23. Schemata 378, n. 24, p. 20.

prayer over the offerings, preface, and prayer after communion are all proper for this Mass.

One special action takes place. When the bishop approaches the altar, he kisses it. He had omitted the kiss at the usual time, the beginning of the Mass, because the altar had not yet been dedicated. These rites of dedication are the only instances when the presider kisses the altar in the middle of the Mass.

The bishop does not incense the gifts, cross, and altar because he has just incensed the newly dedicated altar. This avoids a duplication of incensing the altar but results in no incensation of the cross or gifts.

As the introduction explains, "When the altar has been prepared, the Bishop celebrates the Eucharist, which is the principal part of the whole rite and also the most ancient" (ODCA IV:23). As in ODCA II:17, this same paragraph cites St. John Chrysostom: "This altar is an object of wonder; by nature it is stone, but it is made holy after it receives the Body of Christ."[24]

The bishop receives the gifts at the chair, and ministers take them to the altar. This happens in other ceremonies, such as the ordination of priests. At a typical Mass when the bishop is the celebrant, he receives the gifts "at a convenient place." His chair is convenient for him, but an area near the front pew would be convenient for those bearing the gifts. In either case, he does not go to the altar until the ministers have arranged it (CB 145–146). Receiving the gifts at his chair signifies his role as celebrant and presider of this Eucharist.

The recommended offertory antiphons are unique to this liturgy. The draft suggested the same two antiphons, though in reverse order, to be sung with Psalm 51:17-19, which contains the verse, "My sacrifice to God, a broken spirit: a broken

---

24. The ODCA cites the Migne series of the Greek Fathers: Saint John Chrysostom, *Homilia XX in II Cor.* 3: PG 61, 540.

and humbled heart, O God, you will not spurn." It names the proper inner spirit that motivates outward sacrifices offered upon altars such as this one.

The first antiphon comes from the Sermon on the Mount: "If you offer your gift at the altar, and there recall that your brother has something against you, leave your gift before the altar, go first and be reconciled with your brother, and then you shall come and offer your gift, alleluia" (Matt 5:23-24).

The second antiphon does not close with an alleluia, making it suitable even during Lent. It is the same one recommended in the Roman Gradual. It recounts an early antecedent for dedicating an altar: "Moses consecrated an altar to the Lord, sacrificing victims and offering holocausts upon it. He made an evening sacrifice for a pleasing fragrance to the Lord God in the sight of the children of Israel" (Exod 24:4, 5). Other chants may be sung, but these show the ancient and contemporary uses of an altar, inspiring the people who will celebrate the Eucharist at it in this church.

In this second antiphon, the Latin word for "sacrificing" is the word for which "immolating" is a cognate. ICEL considered a more descriptive phrase, "burning the gifts," but this idea did not advance. The milder translation draws a more immediate parallel to the actual usage of the altar at Mass.

The prayer over the offerings is found first in the ninth-century Gregorian Sacramentary, where it serves as the "Prayer after Covering the Altar" in the dedication ceremony.[25] It appeared in the preconciliar ceremonies for the consecration of an altar just after the bishop incensed it.[26] In that ceremony, the celebration of Mass began after the consecration of the altar, so the prayer occupied a place apart from the Eucharist.

25. Gregorian Sacramentary I:816.
26. PR 1595–1596, p. 441.

Its words remain virtually unchanged today, though they are now positioned as the prayer over the offerings during the Mass. The bishop is required to use it even if this celebration takes place on Christmas, Epiphany, Ascension, Pentecost, or on Sundays of Advent, Lent, and Easter (IV:15). Its invocation of the Holy Spirit secures its place in the overall dedication of the altar: "May your Holy Spirit come down upon this altar, we pray, O Lord our God, to sanctify the gifts of your people and graciously to cleanse the hearts of all who receive them."

The preface is required even on the same days as the prayer over the offerings (IV:15). It demands the use of Eucharistic Prayer I or III because II is for less solemn occasions and IV has its own irreplaceable preface. This new preface was drafted in 1972,[27] and it was only slightly altered before appearing in the final edition of the ritual a few years later. Its style resembles the preface for the dedication of a church, though its content more directly concerns the altar (IV:60).

It calls Christ "the true Priest and the true oblation," recalling Hebrews 5:5-6, which applies to him the appearance of Melchizedek in Psalm 110:4; and Ephesians 5:2, which says Christ handed himself over as a sacrifice. According to St. Paul, Jesus "taught us to celebrate the memorial of the Sacrifice" (1 Cor 11:24-26). By calling this altar "an exalted place," the prayer calls to mind God's promise to Jeremiah that a temple would be established in an exalted city (Jer 30:18-19, 22). As the place where the sacrifice of Christ is "ever offered in mystery," the altar will fulfill God's design that a sacrifice be offered from the rising of the sun to its setting (Mal 1:11). The phrase "Here is prepared the table of the Lord," recalls Psalm 23:5. The people will be "fed by the Body of Christ" at the altar, providing a means for them to realize Jesus' promise that those who

27. Schemata 378, n. 28, p. 21.

eat his flesh will have eternal life (John 6:54-55). The altar provides a place where people "are gathered into the one holy Church," recalling the prophecy of Caiaphas that the death of Jesus would gather the people into one (John 11:51-52). The preface declares that the faithful will drink of the Spirit "from the streams that flow from Christ, the spiritual rock," which combines allusions to passages such as John 7:37-39, where Jesus speaks of the Spirit as the source of life-giving water, and 1 Corinthians 10:4, where Paul says that Christ was the rock that produced water in the desert for thirsty Israel. It also alludes to Isaiah's promise that the people will draw water from the springs of salvation (Isa 12:3).[28] The expectation that the people will become "a living altar" recalls Peter's declaration that the people are living stones (1 Pet 2:5). This rich preface offers an impressive meditation on the biblical roots to the purpose of an altar.

At communion, the order for the dedication of an altar recommends Psalm 128, the same communion chant as Chapter II's order for the dedication of a church. It even borrows one of the antiphons: "Like shoots of the olive, may the children of the Church be gathered around the table of Lord," with a concluding "alleluia" in Easter Time. It therefore repeats Chapter II's insight that the community's gathering at the altar parallels the gathering of a large family at meals.

The first recommended communion antiphon, however, comes from a different psalm: "The sparrow finds a home, and the swallow a nest for her young: By your altars, O Lord of hosts, my King and my God. Blessed are they who dwell in your house, forever singing your praise" (Ps 84:4-5). In Easter Time this antiphon, too, concludes with an alleluia.

28. Ward and Johnson, *The Prefaces of the Roman Missal*, pp. 370-73.

The prayer after communion is the one that appeared in the 1972 draft.[29] It has no clear antecedent in liturgical history and summarizes several themes of the postconciliar renewal. The opening line references Psalm 84:4-5, the joy of dwelling forever near the altar of the Lord. It describes the community as those "united in faith and charity" and prays that "we, who by Christ are nourished, into Christ may be transformed." Even the use of the first-person plural instead of the third person plural gives the prayer a contemporary tone.

The Blessing and Dismissal

The bishop and deacon conduct the concluding rites, alternating lines as usual. The bishop greets and blesses the people, while the deacon asks them to bow and dismisses them (ODCA IV:63–64 and CB 953).

The solemn blessing from the first draft underwent some changes before the typical edition was published. For example, the second element sought a more interior blessing: "And may he who established Christ as the victim and altar of his own sacrifice teach you to offer spiritual sacrifices upon the altar of your heart."[30] This was expanded for a more communitarian message: "And may he, who gathers you at one table and renews you with one Bread, make of you one heart and one soul" (ODCA IV:63).

The original draft had a more expansive rubric at the end: "Lastly, the deacon dismisses the people in the usual way, and all go out giving thanks to God with joy."[31] As in other examples of this, the revisers probably decided that it was difficult to command people how to leave the building. Furthermore,

29. Schemata 378, n. 30, p. 22.
30. Schemata 378, n. 31, p. 22.
31. Schemata 378, n. 32, p. 23.

the Order of Mass oddly never explicitly commands the people to leave, even after the deacon requests it.

Even so, the solemn dedication of a new altar should fill a community with much joy. They have anticipated this day with prayer and sacrifice. They will celebrate in gratitude.

CHAPTER V

The Order of Blessing a Church

This chapter guides the blessing of "oratories, chapels, or sacred buildings which, because of special circumstances, are destined for divine worship only for a time" (ODCA V:1 and CB 954). The diocesan bishop conducts the ceremony, or he may delegate a priest to do so (ODCA V:2 and CB 956). Bugnini comments,

> The rites here are extremely simple. At the blessing of a church, there is no solemn entrance. The sprinkling of the faithful, the altar, and the walls takes place after the greeting and opening address.
>
> After the homily and the general intercessions, there is a prayer of blessing. If the altar is to be dedicated, the dedication is performed at this point.[1]

The blessing may take place on any day except during the Paschal Triduum. On days of special importance (Table of Liturgical Days 1–4), the Mass of the day must be celebrated, but on other days the blessing may take place either during the Mass of the day or within the Mass of the title of the church

---

1. Bugnini, *Reform of the Liturgy*, p. 797.

or oratory; for example, a votive Mass of the Sacred Heart, of the Blessed Virgin Mary, or of some other saint for whom the chapel is named (ODCA V:4 and CB 957).

In some circumstances, the altar of the building will be dedicated (V:6 and CB 959). If so, the pertinent parts of Chapter IV apply.

All the sacred contents of the building are blessed in the one ceremony. The cross, images, organ, and stations of the cross "do not therefore need a special blessing or installation" (CB 954).

Part One: The Introductory Rites

The Entrance into the Church
The gathering of the people and procession take place as at a usual Mass, except that the bishop neither kisses nor incenses the altar when he arrives in the sanctuary (ODCA V:8 and CB 961). The bishop greets the people, using one of the usual formulas or the one that pertains to rites of the dedication of the church and altar: "May grace and peace be with you all in the holy Church of God" (ODCA V:9 and CB 962).

The Blessing and Sprinkling of Water
The bishop blesses the water for sprinkling on the people, "as a sign of repentance and as a remembrance of Baptism," and on the walls to purify them (ODCA V:10 and CB 963).

His opening words draw inspiration from the opening address in the dedication of a church (II:30) and its invitation to prayer before the sprinkling (II:48). However, instead of declaring that the community has come to "dedicate" the church, he says that they have come "to offer a new church to God." He adds, "let us remember that we ourselves, gathered as one in faith and charity, make up the living Church, placed in the world as a sign and witness of the love with which God cares for all people."

The postconciliar committee revising this ceremony released its first draft in February 1972. The introduction proposed at that time has remained in the typical edition with only a few enrichments.[2] The original water blessing, though, was considerably different. In fact, it was a version of the prayer that remains as the collect (V:15). In its place, the prayer of blessing from Chapter II has been copied here.

The bishop sprinkles the people and the walls of the church (V:12–13 and CB 963–964). If the altar is to be dedicated, he also sprinkles it; otherwise, he does not. The people sing, and the antiphons recommended in earlier chapters for this moment are repeated here. To close the sprinkling rite, the bishop offers the same prayer as in the chapter for the dedication of a church (II:50).

The draft had suggested singing Psalm 122 with the antiphon, "We will go rejoicing to the house of the Lord," during the sprinkling, which the rituals of dedication preserve as a hymn of entrance into a new church. However, this recommendation did not remain in the published book, perhaps to draw a distinction between the nature of this building and one that is fully dedicated, or perhaps because the people have already entered the new building before they are sprinkled. The draft had also suggested the classic Latin hymn, "Where Charity and Love Prevail" but permitted other appropriate music.[3] Instead of these suggestions, the ones that pertain to the sprinkling in the other chapters reappear here.

2. Sacra Congregatio pro Cultu Divino, Schemata 380, De Pontificali, n. 28, 15 February 1972, IV:6, p. 2.

3. Schemata 380, IV:8, p. 2.

The Hymn and the Collect

All sing the Gloria, unless the blessing takes place during a Sunday or weekday Mass of Advent or Lent (ODCA V:14 and CB 965). This detail distinguishes this liturgy from the grander dedication of a church and altar. On that occasion, a Mass taking place during Advent and Lent replaces the seasonal liturgy and includes the Gloria (ODCA II:7). If only the altar is dedicated, not the building, then a liturgy celebrated on Sundays of Advent and Lent retains the seasonal celebration, and the Gloria is omitted (ODCA IV:15). Here, for the blessing (not the dedication) of a building, if the event takes place during an Advent or Lent Sunday Mass, the Gloria is omitted. The introduction to this chapter, however, permits a Mass of the Title of the church or oratory even on a weekday of Advent and Lent (II:4). In that case, the Gloria could be sung because the rest of the liturgy pertains to the saint, not to the season. In the regular calendar, the observance of St. Joseph during Lent provides an example of a saint's day that include a Gloria during a penitential season.

The bishop offers the collect of the day if the celebration is among those ranked among the first four numbers of the Table of Liturgical Days. These include seasonal Sundays and all solemnities but not Sundays in Ordinary Time or feasts. On such days of lower rank, the bishop offers the collect special to this liturgy (ODCA V:15 and CB 965).

The collect is very similar to one from the Mass "For a Spiritual or Pastoral Gathering" in the Missal's Masses for Various Needs and Occasions (20). Both prayers ask that the community may become aware of the presence of Jesus Christ, but the one for this ritual Mass adds a petition that the Lord send his blessing "on this church, which you have permitted us to build." Both prayers reference Jesus' promise to be present when two or three have gathered in his name (Matt 18:20). Both are recent additions to the body of prayers in the Catholic church.

Part Two: The Liturgy of the Word

The readings come from the Mass of the day or from the lectionary's Mass for the Rite of the Dedication of a Church. A summary of those pertaining to the rite appears above in the commentary on Chapter Two. The occasions for which the ritual Mass readings may be used are limited to those explained in ODCA V:4.

For the gospel, ministers do not carry incense nor candles. These will play a larger role later in the ceremony. Their absence at this point heightens their anticipation.

The bishop preaches the homily. All recite the creed and the universal prayer in the usual way (ODCA V:16–19 and CB 966). This ceremony does not include a Litany of the Saints that replaces the universal prayer in ceremonies of dedication. If, however, the altar is to be dedicated with the ceremonies of Chapter IV, then the universal prayer is omitted, and the litany is sung (ODCA V:22).

Part Three: The Blessing of the Altar

All may sing as the bishop approaches the altar. He invites the community to join him in prayer. After a period of silence, he prays the blessing. All respond, "Blessed be God for ever." He incenses the altar. A minister incenses the bishop and then walks around to incense the people and the nave (ODCA V:20–21 and CB 967).

There are exceptions. If the altar is to be dedicated, then the material from Chapter IV is used, including the Litany of the Saints. On the other hand, if the altar has already been blessed, then it is not blessed again (ODCA V:22 and CB 968). For example, the community may have installed an older altar, previously dedicated in another space, into its chapel.

The antiphon suggested to open the ceremony is one of the recommended communion antiphons from the orders of dedication of a church or an altar (ODCA II:78 and IV:61). "Like shoots of the olive" is usually paired with Psalm 128. As usual, another antiphon may be sung at this time.

The bishop's invitation to prayer is unique to this ceremony because the other ones enlist the people's assistance in the Litany of the Saints. Here he asks their assistance in the simple prayer of blessing: "Let us join in this rite with attentive spirit, asking God to look kindly on the Church's offering that will be placed on this altar, and make of his people an eternal offering to himself." The language recalls Eucharistic Prayer III, where the celebrant prays that the community may be made "an eternal offering" to God (Order of Mass 113) and responds to Paul's admonition that Christians make their bodies a living sacrifice (Rom 12:1).

The prayer of blessing is a simplified version of the one for the dedication of an altar. The history of this rite extends back through the Pontificals of 1961[4] and 1595–1596,[5] all the way to the thirteenth-century Pontifical of Durandus.[6] These orders of service described elaborate ceremonies that included the sprinkling and anointing of "portable altars." In 1965, the first gathering of a committee to discuss the revised pontifical after the Council's Constitution on the Sacred Liturgy posed a new direction: "It is asked whether finally the rite of consecration of a portable altar, as it currently exists in the new [1961] Pontifical, may be further simplified?"[7]

---

4. PR 1961, pp. 180–88.
5. PR 1595–1596, pp. 444–60.
6. Durand II IV, pp. 498–504.
7. Schemata 67, n. 6, p. 3.

This chapter on the blessing of a church appears in the ODCA before the chapter for the blessing of an altar, but the latter was drafted first. Elements of it have been brought into this one. The first draft of the revised liturgy in 1972 called for a "movable altar" to be endowed with a special blessing, not a consecration or dedication.[8] "In the base of the altar, however, it is not permitted to inter the relics of saints."[9]

The same draft recommended that the people, not just the bishop, gather at the altar, singing the antiphon still recommended for the ceremony, "Like shoots of the olive, may the children of the Church be gathered around the table of the Lord." The draft for the bishop's invitation to prayer stressed the priesthood of the people: "A holy people, which you are, gathering around one altar, draws near to Christ, the living stone, in whom it grows into a holy temple, and, exercising a royal priesthood, offers to God upon the altar of their heart the pleasing and acceptable sacrifice of a life carried out in holiness."[10] The draft of the bishop's prayer is a somewhat simpler version of the one preserved in the ritual today.[11]

That current prayer borrows many of the ideas from the *preface* for the Mass of the dedication of an altar (IV:60), but it is less solemn and stripped of most of its biblical allusions. It connects the use of an altar to the sacrifice of Christ on the cross. It prays that the altar may be "the center of . . . praise and thanksgiving," where the "bread of life" is broken (John 6:48) and believers "drink of the cup of unity," which is "the fountain from which flows an unending stream of salvation" (Isa 12:3 and John 7:37-39), enabling those who draw near

8. Schemata 380, V:1, p. 4.
9. Schemata 380, V:3, p. 4.
10. Schemata 380, V:7, p. 5.
11. Schemata 380, V:8, p. 5.

"to Christ, the living stone" (1 Pet 2:4) to "grow in him into a holy temple" (1 Pet 2:5), offering on the altar of their heart "the sacrifice of a life spent in holiness, pleasing and acceptable" (V:21). Thus, the final version of the prayer borrowed some of the imagery originally placed in the bishop's introduction to it.

The bishop does not anoint the altar with chrism, as the historical antecedents of this rite had him do. This further distinguishes this blessing from a dedication.

Part Four: The Liturgy of the Eucharist

Ministers cover the altar with its cloth. They may decorate it with flowers and candles, and a cross, if necessary. The bishop receives the gifts from representatives of the faithful at his chair. All may sing an antiphon (ODCA V:23–24 and CB 969). The liturgy recommends the same ones for the dedication of an altar (ODCA IV:57): "If you offer your gifts," and "Moses consecrated an altar."

The first draft of the blessing of a movable altar had a different antiphon in place, "Christ the Lord, Priest forever according to the order of Melchizedek, offered bread and wine."[12] Repositioning here the other antiphons lends more coherence to the book, especially since one would associate the image of Christ as priest with a different ceremony: the anointing of a dedicated altar.

The bishop approaches the altar and kisses it for the first time in this Mass. He deferred the kiss that usually concludes the entrance procession until he has blessed the altar. Because he has just incensed the altar, he does not incense the altar, the cross and the gifts (ODCA V:25 and CB 970).

12. Schemata 380, V:10, p. 6.

If there is a chapel for the Blessed Sacrament in the church being blessed, the bishop inaugurates it after communion (ODCA V:26 and CB 970), following the procedure from the full order of the dedication of a church (ODCA II:79–82).

The bishop and the deacon conduct the blessing and dismissal (ODCA V:27–28). The blessing is the same formula from the order of the dedication of the church with the change of a single word: from the "dedication" of this church to the "blessing" of this church (ODCA II:84 and CB 971).

Overall, the ceremony of blessing is a simplified yet meaningful version of the one for a dedication, honoring the new space for worship, but implying its relatively secondary importance to a dedicated church.

CHAPTER VI

The Order of Blessing an Altar

A movable altar differs from a fixed one, yet because it is designated for the celebration of the Eucharist, it is blessed before put to use. A fixed altar, the main altar of a church, is to be dedicated; a movable altar is blessed. Even the Missal distinguishes between the dedication of a fixed altar and the blessing of a moveable one (GIRM 300). A fixed altar may include relics of saints; a movable altar may not. The movable altar is appropriately blessed by the bishop or the rector of the church. It may be blessed on any day except Good Friday and Holy Saturday. The prayers and readings come from the Mass of the day (ODCA VI:1–7 and CB 972–978). Such an altar may be built of "any noble and solid material suited to liturgical use" (GIRM 301).

After the universal prayer, the bishop goes to the altar. All may sing an antiphon; "Like shoots of the olive" is recommended (ODCA VI:8 and CB 979). This is the communion antiphon for the Masses of dedication of a church and of an altar (ODCA II:78 and IV:61), and it is the antiphon used at the same moment in the order of blessing a church (V:20). As mentioned above, the first draft of this liturgy permitted the people to begin the Mass gathered at the altar together with the bishop.[1]

---

1. Schemata 380, V:6, p. 4.

The bishop's invitation is almost identical to the one used for the blessing of a church (V:21). The only difference is that he unsurprisingly announces that the community has gathered "to bless this altar" (VI:9), not "to bless this church." The prayer of blessing is identical to the one from the previous chapter's blessing of the church, which includes a blessing of the altar.

The bishop sprinkles the altar with blessed water and incenses it. A minister incenses the bishop and then the people. Ministers cover the altar with a cloth and may decorate it, arranging the candles and, if necessary, a cross. All may sing, "If you offer your gift," as in the blessing of a church, or another antiphon. The bishop approaches the altar, kisses it, and Mass continues as usual, though without an incensation of the altar and the gifts (ODCA VI:10–13 and CB 980–983).

This is a simplified version of the already simplified blessing of a church. Only those elements pertaining to the blessing of the altar remain.

As mentioned above, a draft of this liturgy from 1972 exists. Elements of it were brought into the previous chapter for blessing a church, on the assumption that the new church or oratory would also have an altar to be blessed. Of some interest, the first draft envisioned a different antiphon, as noted above: "Christ the Lord, Priest forever according to the order of Melchizedek, offered bread and wine."[2] The antiphon that appears in the typical edition focuses more on the community gathered around the altar, "Like shoots of the olive."

The first draft also proposed a different sequence for the incensation of the altar, similar to the one under consideration for the dedication of a church. It deferred the incensation until the preparation of the gifts after the altar was prepared and the bishop had kissed it. The altar and gifts were therefore to be

2. Schemata 380, V:10, p. 6.

incensed at the moment when this happens at any Mass with incense.[3] In the end, the incensation moved closer to the bishop's prayer of blessing as a particular sign of the sacredness of the altar. Now when the gifts are set upon the altar a few minutes later, they are not incensed to avoid overusing the same symbol.

In all, the liturgy of blessing an altar is quite simple. Not only is the order of service minimal, the presider may be a priest, even without the bishop's delegation. The blessing has no impact on the presider's prayers or on the Scripture readings associated with the Mass of the day. Still, it serves the important purpose of blessing the central furnishing for eucharistic worship.

3. Schemata 380, V:11, p. 6.

CHAPTER VII

The Order of Blessing a Chalice and a Paten

I t may seem odd that a ritual book focusing on churches and altars includes a chapter on the blessing of a chalice and a paten. However, in the history of these rituals, a series of ceremonies formed a kind of appendix to the orders of consecration, dedication, and blessing.

The Roman-Germanic Pontifical of the tenth century, for example, added orders for the blessing of altar cloths, vessels, and instruments used at church, including a cross and censers, as well as an order for dedicating a baptistry and consecrating a cemetery.[1]

The Roman Pontifical of the twelfth century appended several ceremonies to the chapters pertaining to the church and altar: the blessing of a chasuble, dalmatic, stole, and other vestments for priests and deacons; and the blessing of a corporal, paten, ciborium, chalice, incense, and new cross.[2]

The twelfth-century Pontifical of the Roman Curia added a blessing of a cemetery, a consecration of a paten and a chalice,

---

1. PRG XL:74–119, pp. 150–66; LII–LV, pp. 190–94.
2. *Pontifical romain au Moyen Âge, Tome I, XII*, XX–XXVI, pp. 201–5.

and a blessing of corporals, a new cross, incense, and of a chasuble, dalmatic, stole, and other vestments for priests and deacons.[3]

The thirteenth-century Pontifical of Durandus adjoined the blessing of a cemetery, vestments, altar cloths, corporals, a new cross, an image of blessed Mary, images of saints, a censer, sacred vessels and ornaments in general, reliquaries, ciboriums, baptistries, and bells.[4]

The Roman Pontifical revised after the Council of Trent had the blessing of a cemetery, of a paten and chalice, vestments, altar cloths, corporals, a new cross, a pectoral cross, an image of the Blessed Virgin Mary, vessels, and ornaments in general, a tabernacle, reliquaries, and bells.[5]

The 1961 pontifical added a blessing for a cemetery, a consecration of a paten and a chalice, the blessing of altar cloths and vessels, a corporal, a pall, a purificator, a new cross, a pectoral cross, an image of the Blessed Virgin Mary and other saints, reliquaries, water, and incense.[6] All these blessings were reserved for bishops.

The 1963 Constitution on the Sacred Liturgy, however, said, "Reserved blessings should be very few, and they should be reserved only to bishops or ordinaries" (79). When the first committee appointed to review the Roman Pontifical met in 1965, the members sorted through the portion of its table of contents dealing with all these ceremonies. They recommended transferring several of them out of the pontifical, thereby allowing priests to bless a tabernacle, ciboriums, monstrances,

3. *Pontifical romain au Moyen Âge, Tome II, Pontifical de la Curie Romaine*, XXIV, pp. 440–41; XXVIII–XXXIII, pp. 449–52.

4. Durand II V, VIII–XXII pp. 504–10, 518–36.

5. PR 1595–1596, pp. 460–79, 496–536.

6. PR 1961 pp. 193–227.

pyxes, altar cloths, the corporal, pall, purificator (which it mistakenly predicted would be omitted,) priestly vestments, other garments, a new cross, an image of the Blessed Virgin Mary, images of the saints, reliquaries, and water.

This preliminary work in 1965 then moved several blessings to the appendix of the pontifical, thus reserving them for bishops: sacred vessels and ornaments of the church or altar, the pectoral cross, Gregorian water, incense; the altar cloths, vessels, and ornaments when the church and altar are blessed at the same time; the cloths, vessels and ornaments when only the altar is consecrated.

Therefore, the first outline for revising this section of the pontifical presented only these orders of service: dedicating and consecrating a church; blessing a church; consecrating an altar without a church dedication; consecrating a portable altar; consecrating the bell; and blessing an antimins, or "Greek corporal," which the 1961 pontifical called "a cloth in place of the altar stone used by apostolic indult in the celebration of Mass."[7] The antimins is no longer required for the celebration of Mass outside a sacred space (GIRM 297).

Many blessings were thus reassigned out of the pontifical and into the Book of Blessings, a collection of prayers for priests, deacons, and laypersons. The first revised draft of this part of the pontifical kept an elaborate blessing of a cemetery,[8] but this too was removed from the typical edition.

All that remains is the blessing of a chalice and paten. These vessels for the Eucharist therefore carry a more elevated presence than other items such as vestments, auxiliary furnishings, and altar cloths. The retention of their blessing in the ODCA shows their dignified place in the Catholic Mass.

7. PR 1961, p. 208.
8. Schemata 380, IX, pp. 1–6.

Furthermore, "When a church is dedicated, such appointments as its baptismal font, cross, images and statues, organ, bells, [and] stations of the cross are to be considered as blessed and duly erected or installed; they therefore need no further blessing, erection, or installation" (CB 864). Even though a priest may bless such items, the bishop's dedication of the church embraces them all. This coheres with the understanding applied to the ambo and the chapel of reservation: the first usage constitutes blessing.

As the Introduction to this chapter says, "Since the chalice and paten are used for the offering and consecration of the bread and wine and for communion, they are reserved exclusively and permanently for the celebration of the Eucharist, and so become 'sacred vessels'" (ODCA VII:1). Although this chapter concludes a book considered part of a bishop's pontifical, any priest may bless a chalice and paten (ODCA VII:3). He may do so within Mass or outside Mass, though the former is preferred (CB 984–986).

In the 1961 pontifical, the bishop consecrated these vessels apart from Mass with a series of prayers. He held the paten first, dipping his thumb in chrism and spreading the sacred oil across the paten from side to side. Then he prayed over the chalice. He dipped his thumb again in chrism and anointed the vessel from lip to lip. A priest dried the vessels with a piece of bread, disposing of it in fire or in the sacrarium.[9] In the previous pontifical, the bishop anointed the entire paten and interior of the chalice, then sprinkled them with blessed water.[10] The revision no longer uses chrism in the consecrating of vessels, minimizing the need for a bishop to preside.

9. PR 1961, pp. 207–8.
10. PR 1595–1596, pp. 496–99.

The Order of Blessing to Be Used within Mass

This order of blessing now also appears in Appendix IV of the third edition of the Roman Missal. The Missal's second edition was published before the ODCA had been completed. The new Missal's appendix includes the introduction (ODCA VII:1-4) but omits the recommended readings (VII:6-8). Everything else is the same. The Missal contains only the rubrics and texts pertaining to the celebration of a Mass, so its appendix does not present the alternative version of blessing the vessels outside Mass. That only appears in this final chapter of the ODCA.

Within Mass, special readings are permitted only on days outside of those ranked 1 through 9 in the Table of Liturgical Days. This basically limits the proclamation of these readings to weekdays outside of Lent that are not obligatory memorials with their own proper readings (ODCA VII:5 and CB 988). The appropriate passages are found in the lectionary from 823 through 826.

The first reading may come from Paul's First Letter to the Corinthians. Two options are offered. The first calls the cup of blessing a participation in the blood of Christ (10:14-22a). The second recounts the events of the Last Supper as Paul once learned them and now passes them along (11:23-26). These readings bear the earliest testimony to Christian usage of a eucharistic chalice.

Psalm 16:5 and 8, 9-10, 11 and Psalm 23:1-3a, 3b-4, 5, 6 are recommended because both have a verse mentioning a cup. In the first, the Lord is compared to a prized cup; in the second, an overflowing cup characterizes the banquet that the Lord prepares. Each of them seems to prophesy the Christian usage of an invaluable vessel brimming with blessing.

For the alleluia verse and verse before the gospel, the lectionary recommends two options from the sixth chapter of John, Jesus' discourse on the Bread of Life: verse 56, where he promises that those who eat his flesh and drink his blood remain in him, and verse 57, where he promises that those who feed on him will have life because of him. This shifts the imagery from the chalice toward the paten, the vessel that will serve the bread of life to those accepting the invitation of Christ.

Choices for the gospel are Matthew 20:20-28, in which Jesus predicts that his followers will share his chalice, referring to destiny of his passion; and Mark 14:12-16, 22-26, the account of sharing the cup at the Last Supper. Both of these hearten today's believers: drinking the chalice advances them through suffering toward salvation.

Except for the gospel acclamations, the recommended readings all focus on the purpose of the chalice, rather than the paten. Only one or two readings are proposed; the occasion does not merit the same attention given the Liturgy of the Word on Sundays with its three readings.

After the proclamation of the Word of God, the homily, and the universal prayer, ministers or representatives of the community place the vessels on the altar. As the priest goes there, all may sing; recommended is the antiphon (Ps 116:13), "The chalice of salvation I will raise, and I will call on the name of the Lord" (VII:10 and CB 989–990). This was suggested even in the first draft of this ceremony from 1972.[11]

At the altar, the priest offers the prayer that declares how these vessels will be blessed: "may the Body and Blood of your Son, offered and received by means of these vessels, make them holy." Not the priest's blessing, but the eucharistic usage of these vessels, makes them holy. The priest then asks God on behalf of the people that "we may be renewed by your Sacraments on earth and endowed with your Spirit, until with the Saints we come to delight in your banquet in the Kingdom of heaven" (VII:11 and CB 991). The prayer thus looks forward not

---

11. Schemata 380, VII:4, p. 1.

only to the rest of the celebration of this Eucharist but toward the eschatological banquet that it foreshadows.

This prayer is an edited version of the one that appeared in the postconciliar commission's first draft. At the beginning, it called the vessel for drinking a "precious chalice," borrowing an adjective from the First Eucharistic Prayer. The ending expanded the imagery of the banquet: "until we drink of that fruit of the vine that Jesus promised to drink new with us in the kingdom of heaven," alluding to Matthew 26:29.[12] These sentiments were redrafted for the typical edition.

After this, ministers place the corporal on the altar; some of the faithful bring forward the bread, wine, and water for the celebration; and the priest leads the usual preparation of the gifts, handling the newly blessed vessels. Meanwhile, all may sing; the recommended antiphon is a modified version of the one that opened the rite: "The chalice of salvation I will raise, and I will offer a sacrifice of praise." An Alleluia is added during Easter Time. Other verses of Psalm 116 may alternate with the antiphon (VII:12 and CB 992).

The first draft proposed a different antiphon with the same psalm: "After the Lord Jesus had eaten, he took the chalice, and, giving thanks, gave it to his disciples."[13] This more direct reference to the Last Supper would have inspired those planning to drink from the chalice, but the psalm verse suffices.

The incensation of the altar and vessels is recommended. The faithful may receive the Blood of Christ from the newly blessed chalice (VII:13–14 and CB 993–994).

The Order of Blessing To Be Used Outside Mass
Outside Mass, the liturgy may begin by singing Psalm 116, as recommended during the preparation of the gifts in the same

---

12. Schemata 380, VII:5, pp. 1–2.
13. Schemata 380, VII:8, p. 2.

order of blessing within Mass. The priest may use any approved greeting of the people, but a special one is proposed: "The grace of our Lord Jesus Christ, who offered his Body and Blood for our salvation, and the love of God, and the communion of the Holy Spirit, be with you all" (VII:15–16).

The priest introduces the ceremony. One or more of the readings from sections 823–826 of the lectionary described above may be proclaimed. In place of the responsorial psalm, all may observe a period of silence. The priest gives a homily (VII:17–19).

Then, before the intercessions, ministers or representatives of the community place the vessels on the altar. All may sing, and the proposed antiphon from the ceremony within Mass is also recommended here (Ps 116:13).

The prayer of the priest differs from the one within Mass. In this case, he explicitly blesses the vessels because they will not immediately be used for the Eucharist. He says, "May these vessels, which, by the consent of your people, are intended for the celebration of the sacrifice of the new covenant, be made holy by your blessing." To complement his words, he makes the sign of the cross over the vessels, which he does not do when the blessing takes place within Mass (VII:21).

The universal prayer follows. This may be freely composed, but a set of intercessions is suggested. The priest's introduction recalls that Jesus gives himself as the bread of life and the chalice of salvation, alluding to John 6:35 and Psalm 116:13. The people may respond, "Christ, heavenly Bread, give us eternal life." The petitions address Christ by a variety of titles: "Savior of us all," "Priest of the Most High," "Good Shepherd," "Lamb of God," and "Son of God." The first petition recalls that the Savior "in obedience to the will of the Father drank the chalice of suffering for our salvation," referring to Matthew 26:35. The purposes of the intercessions range from having the community become "sharers in the mystery" of the death of Christ to asking God "that we may draw from the mystery of the Eucharist a love for you and for all people" (VII:22).

The priest invites all to offer the Lord's Prayer with an introduction that interprets the passion of Christ as an example, fulfillment, and instruction: "Nailed to the Cross, Christ became the Mediator of salvation and by fulfilling the Father's will, he taught us how to pray." The priest concludes by asking God to "preserve in us the work of your mercy" (VII:22). He blesses and dismisses the people as usual (VII:23). No mention is made of a deacon, but if one is present, he would logically proclaim the gospel and dismiss the people.

That final prayer is almost identical to two others in the liturgy. One is the Missal's collect for a Votive Mass of the Most Precious Blood of Our Lord Jesus Christ. The other is a prayer at Benediction of the Most Blessed Sacrament, found in Holy Communion and Worship of the Eucharist Outside Mass (229). It was added to this ceremony sometime after the first draft in 1972.

Conclusion

The General Instruction of the Roman Missal outlines the ordinary usage of a dedicated church. It describes the altar and its ornamentation in 296–308. It calls the altar—on which the Sacrifice of the Cross is effected under sacramental signs—the table of Lord where the people of God gather and participate at Mass. "It is also the center of the thanksgiving that is accomplished through the Eucharist" (296).

For this reason, the GIRM limits what may be placed on top of the altar from the beginning of Mass: A cross is placed on or near the altar; candlesticks are placed either on the altar or around it (307); the book of the gospels may rest there (306). For the Liturgy of the Eucharist, elements on top of the altar are limited to "the chalice with the paten, a ciborium, if necessary, and, finally, the corporal, the purificator, the pall, and the Missal" (306). Other items do not belong on the mensa, and after one has witnessed the consecration of an altar with chrism, one understands this better.

As Calabuig notes in the conclusion to his commentary, the dedication of a church is a pageant of many temples: the cosmic dwelling of God, the tents of the Exodus, the Jerusalem temple, the temple that is Christ in whom the Spirit fully dwells, the gathered people who are called the church, each member of them, and their destiny, the new Jerusalem. "This great pageant is brought together and evoked in the temple of stone, the smallest of them all, whose glory is to be a sign and a reverberation of the glory of the others." Calabuig also quotes Pope St. Paul VI: "If a church is the place of the divine presence, this place is the assembly of the faithful, is the soul of each believer."[14]

When a community gathers to begin construction, to dedicate or bless a church or an altar, even to bless the vessels for worship, the members are expressing faith in God, whose presence especially inhabits designated places. They also express their identity as the people of God, who become visibly one within that sacred space. Especially after celebrating the construction of a new building, they have symbolically only laid its foundation stone. They prove themselves to be a generation of Christians filled with faith who used their resources to provide a home for God and for their children, a place with whom they share a title: church.

14. Calabuig, "Commentary," p. 36.

Two Solemnities
on the Parish Calendar

The Anniversary of Dedication and the Title of the Church

The dedication of a church adds two solemnities to the parish calendar: the anniversary of the dedication and the Title of the church. These rank in the Table of Liturgical Days under level 4, Proper Solemnities. It may surprise parishioners and staff alike that the observance of such solemnities outranks many feasts and Sundays of the liturgical year, even governing the readings and prayers in use for occasions such as confirmations and weddings.

For this reason, the dedication may not take place on any day that ranks among levels 1 through 3 on the Table of Liturgical Days. This eliminates days such as the Triduum; Christmas; Epiphany; Ascension; Pentecost; Sundays of Advent, Lent, and Easter; solemnities already on the calendar; and All Souls' Day. Those days outrank both the dedication of the church and its anniversary.

If the anniversary falls on a day such as a Sunday in Ordinary Time or a weekday in Lent, it takes over the liturgy. The presidential prayers and readings come from the section of the

Missal and lectionary for the anniversary of the dedication of the parish church.

The parish has some flexibility, especially during Ordinary Time. It may celebrate its anniversary on the date itself or on a nearby Sunday. Usually this is the Sunday in Ordinary Time closest to the date in question, though paragraph 58 of the Universal Norms for the Liturgical Year and Calendar does not so limit the choice.

The parish also has the option of celebrating its anniversary on the Sunday before November 1. If the anniversary date is not known, the bishop may assign it either to the Sunday before November 1 or to October 25, which serves as a catchall date for anniversaries of dedications.[1] Such a date shows the connection between the dedication of the building and the earthly church's devotion to the heavenly church of saints.

Similarly, the Title of the church becomes a solemnity. Some Titles are already solemnities on the calendar, such as the Immaculate Conception, Sts. Peter and Paul, and the Sacred Heart. This results in no net change for the parish's annual celebration of its Title.

In other cases, however, the Title of the church raises the annual observance to a solemnity. This affects days such as St. Andrew, Our Lady of Guadalupe, the Immaculate Heart of Mary, St. Louis, and St. Cecilia, to name only a few.

In some dioceses, parishes have closed, and communities have joined together. Sometimes the diocese assigns a new name for the community of merged parishes. For example, closing a church called Holy Trinity may cause the parishioners to merge with a parish that gathers at the church of St. Stephen, but the newly merged community receives a new name,

---

1. "*Documentorum explanatio: De Celebratione annuali dedicationis ecclesiae*," *Notitiae* 8 71/3 (March 1972): 103.

such as Our Lady of Peace. Even so, the continued use of the church building that was dedicated to St. Stephen means that the Parish of Our Lady of Peace observes each year the titular solemnity of its church on Stephen's feast, December 26. The Title of the church cannot be changed.

As with the anniversary of dedication, the parish may celebrate its titular solemnity on a Sunday in Ordinary Time. This falls under the same provisions of the Universal Norms for the Liturgical Year and Calendar (58).

In some years, the anniversary may fall on a day of greater rank. For example, a church dedicated in April may occasionally find its anniversary on a Sunday in Easter Time. That Sunday, at level 3 of the Table of Liturgical Days, outranks the dedication anniversary, which then moves to the next open day on the calendar, usually Monday that year. Because the anniversary is a solemnity, it must be observed each year.

If the church was dedicated on its own titular day, then the solemnities are observed on consecutive days. The anniversary at 4b on the Table of Liturgical Days nudges out the titular observance at 4c. It creates the somewhat lamentable circumstance that the parish celebrates its Title on the day after the rest of the Catholic world. It is more advisable to choose a different day for the dedication. This is one reason that churches may not be dedicated on days that rank in levels 1–3 on the Table.

These solemnities pertain to a dedicated church. Therefore, they relate to Chapters II and III of the ODCA. They do not pertain to the ceremonies of beginning the construction (I), the dedication of an altar inside a previously dedicated church (IV), or the blessing of a church or altar (V and VI). The anniversary of the blessing of an oratory, for example, does not share the rank of the anniversary of the dedication of a parish church. An anniversary of blessing has no impact on the assigned liturgical day.

The Anniversary Liturgy

The annual celebration of the dedication of its church provides an occasion for gathering the community. As time goes by, fewer people who attended the dedication of a modern church are alive; in historic parishes, all of them are ancestors from the ever-dimming recesses of the past. Each year, succeeding generations honor the purpose of this holy space when they thank God for the witness of the initial community who sacrificed to build the church.

The parish celebration may take place at a time when the community may gather socially as well. Families may welcome ideas that bring the celebration into their homes: a prayer at mealtime, for example, or upon waking or going to bed. Information about the building, its art, and its purposes may be retold. Neighbors and visitors may be invited to tour the building and its grounds. The anniversary day deserves local celebration in a variety of ways.

For the Mass, a solemnity requires the addition of the Gloria and the Creed, the proclamation of three Scripture readings as on Sundays, and the use of special presidential prayers. These come from the first subsection of the Roman Missal entitled "Commons." A note at the beginning reminds the reader that the actual Mass of Dedication is found in a completely different section, the Ritual Masses, where it occupies the last place.

This first of the commons itself divides into two parts, both pertaining to an anniversary of dedication. The first concerns celebrations "In the Church That was Dedicated" and the second to those "Outside the Church That was Dedicated." The most common use of the second category is the annual anniversary of the dedication of one's diocesan cathedral, which ranks as a feast, level 8b on the Table of Liturgical Days, in all the parishes outside the cathedral, where, of course, it is a solemnity. As a feast in a parish, the Mass for the anniversary of the cathedral's dedication requires the Gloria, but not the Creed; two readings, not three.

A related celebration is the Dedication of the Lateran Basilica, a feast on November 9 throughout the Catholic world—except at the Lateran Basilica in Rome, where it ranks as a solemnity. Because that cathedral is the mother church of the entire Catholic world, every parish celebrates the feast of its universal cathedral. When November 9 falls on a Sunday, this feast, considered a feast of the Lord, replaces the Sunday in Ordinary Time.

Of present interest is the common of dedication "In the Church That was Dedicated," the parish's own solemnity. The proper antiphons and presidential prayers are the first ones listed among the Missal's commons.

The readings for this Mass are found in a comparable place in the fourth volume of the lectionary. The commons appear at the beginning of that volume, and the readings for the dedication anniversary are first among them.

Entrance Antiphon

The recommended entrance antiphon for the Mass of dedication is Psalm 68:36, "Wonderful are you, O God in your holy place. The God of Israel himself gives his people strength and courage. Blessed be God!" If the anniversary falls during Easter Time, the antiphon concludes with an alleluia. This is the same entrance antiphon recommended for the dedication of a church already in use (Chapter III).

Psalm 68 in its entirety celebrates the protection that the people receive from God, who drives away enemies, provides for the needy, showers rain, and favors the city of Jerusalem. The antiphon for the Mass is the last verse of this psalm, summing up the reason for the people's joy: God dwells within the temple of the holy city. Singing this verse inside a church on the anniversary of its dedication celebrates the divine presence within this holy space and acknowledges God's protection over those who worship there.

The introit from the Roman Gradual instead has Genesis 28:17 and 22, together with the two opening verses of Psalm 84. The first of the verses from Genesis comes from an optional first reading from the lectionary's Ritual Mass for the Dedication of an Altar. The full passage recounts Jacob's vision of a ladder that joins earth to heaven and his decision to anoint a stone to mark the place.

Psalm 84 appears frequently in the ODCA. It is recommended for the Approach to the Place Where the Church Is to Be Built (I:14), when anointing the altar and walls of the church (II:64 and III:24), The Entrance into the Church for the Dedication of an Altar (IV:33), and a responsorial psalm option in the lectionary for the dedication of an altar (819.1).

The Simple Gradual proposes this introit: "I will go up to your house, O Lord, and I will adore at your holy temple." This pairs with Psalm 5, a prayer about praying. One verse says, "I enter your house. I bow down before your holy temple, in awe of you." The final verses of this psalm serve as the offertory in the Roman Gradual's Common of Martyrs and of Holy Men and Women: "in you they rejoice, those who love your name. It is you who bless the just one, O LORD; you surround him with your favor like a shield." This connection to the saints who love the Lord's name and whom the Lord protects strengthens the appropriateness of this entrance antiphon, especially if the relics of a saint have been set beneath the altar. If the church had been dedicated in the preconciliar era, a schola led the Litany of the Saints as the ministers entered the building.

Another suitable song may replace these. Best would be one that shares these purposes, gathering the people in praise of God for their sacred space.

Collect

The collect for the anniversary comes from the eighth-century Gelasian Gellone Sacramentary. A slightly longer version of the same prayer filled this place in the preconciliar Roman Missal.

The priest praises God who brings the anniversary day to the community, and he prays for two correlated intentions: "that in this place for you there may always be pure worship and for us, fullness of redemption." The people gathered for this Mass are not just praying selfishly for their own redemption, but that their building may be a place of pure worship.

These intentions allude to two biblical passages. In reference to God, the words recall Malachi 1:11, where God commanded a pure sacrifice to his name from the rising to the setting of the sun. The early section of Eucharistic Prayer III includes a phrase that refers to the same prophecy (Order of Mass 108).

The request for the people's "fullness of redemption" borrows vocabulary from Psalm 130:7, a plea for salvation made by those who cry for forgiveness, out of the depths. This petition implies that the people are familiar with this psalm of repentance. Their contrite humility makes them more capable of offering the pure sacrifice that God requests.

The Liturgy of the Word

The five options for a first reading from the Old Testament are in the Lectionary for Mass 701. The first is the prayer of Solomon at the dedication of the temple he had constructed in Jerusalem (1 Kgs 8:22-23, 27-30). His ancient prayer served as the model for the prayer of dedication for a new church (ODCA II:62). Solomon stood before the altar and stretched his hands toward heaven in a gesture that presiders still imitate when praying publicly before God. As the contemporary community celebrates the anniversary of the dedication of its church, this passage reminds them of the long history of believers who designated spaces for sacred worship.

At the dedication of the temple, Solomon summoned the leaders of the community to process the ark of the covenant from the City of David into the new building. The passage from 2 Chronicles 5:6-10, 13–6:2 tells of the sacrifices offered before the ark and the description of its contents. As the contemporary community prays within the church on its anniversary day, this second option for the first reading recalls the first usage of the temple of Jerusalem for solemn worship.

In the third option, the Lord commands the people through the prophet to act justly (Isa 56:1, 6-7). If they keep the covenant, even if they are foreigners, God will accept their sacrifices in the temple. This passage reminds the contemporary community that they must be people of noble character in order to offer a worthy sacrifice and that their church is to be a house of prayer for all.

The people in exile yearning to return home to Jerusalem and their temple heard a hopeful prophecy. Their destroyed place of worship needed to be rebuilt, but Ezekiel sees in a vision the glory of the Lord entering the temple once again (Ezek 43:1-2, 3c-7a). On the anniversary of the dedication of their church, this fourth option for the first reading makes parishioners mindful of the presence of the glory of the Lord that they have experienced in this holy place.

Also from the prophet Ezekiel, the fifth option provides a vision of water flowing from the restored temple in Jerusalem (47:1-2, 8-9, 12). Today's community celebrates the anniversary of the building in which previous generations received sacramental grace flowing from font and table.

During Easter Time, the first reading comes from one of three possibilities in the New Testament (Lectionary 702). The two from the book of Revelation were treated above in Chapter II:54 because they replace the *second* reading for the dedication of a new church when the ritual takes place in Easter Time. The third option comes from the final sermon of St. Stephen in Acts of the Apostles (7:44-50). Stephen outlines a brief history of the houses of God: Moses's tent of testimony in the desert and the building of Solomon's temple. Stephen then cites Isaiah 66:1-2, in order to show that the Lord does not require an earthly building. He sees a vision of Jesus within God's dwelling place in the heavens, essentially inviting his listeners to find in Christ the fulfillment of the temple. This leads directly to Stephen's martyrdom. The passage reminds the contemporary community that their entire church building is but a symbol of the heavenly dwelling place of God and of the command to bear witness to Christ, even in the face of persecution.

The lectionary offers five options for the responsorial psalm (703). The first is a canticle sung by King David at the end of his life, anticipating that his son Solomon will construct the temple of David's dreams (1 Chr 29:10, 11, 12, with 13b as the refrain). This succinct hymn of praise reappears as a communion hymn in the Simple Gradual for occasions such as the solemnities of the Most Holy Trinity and of Our Lord Jesus Christ the King of the Universe. The community singing it on the anniversary of the dedication of its church continues the original purpose of the building: giving praise to the glorious name of God.

The second option, Psalm 46:2-3, 5-6, 8-9, proclaims the presence of God in the holy city. In the liturgy, this responsorial selects a refrain about the stream that gladdens the city of God, prophesying the waters of baptism that bring joy to Christians gathered in a holy place. In the Bible, the psalm has its own refrain declaring that the Lord of Hosts is with the people who sing it. Both in the Bible and in the liturgy, this psalm celebrates the presence of God amid the people gathered in his holy dwelling place.

Psalm 84:3, 4, 5 and 10, 11 is the pilgrimage song much in use throughout the ODCA. It expresses the joy of those making a

holy journey to a sacred place. On the lips of Christians inside
their house of worship, it echoes the happy sentiments of believers past.

The fourth option, Psalm 95:1-2, 3-5, 6-7 invites the people
to come before the Lord to praise him. It exhorts the faithful
to assume postures for worship: bowing down and kneeling
before the Lord. The people singing it today recall that their
habits of worship performed in their dedicated church have
ancestry deep in the history of believers.

The final option for the responsorial is Psalm 122:1-2, 3-4ab,
8-9. As with Psalm 84, the ODCA regards this as another beloved processional hymn. For example, all may sing it upon
entering the building for the first time. Originally a pilgrimage
song to the Jerusalem temple, it still cheers the faithful preparing to encounter God in a holy dwelling place.

Usually, a cantor will lead one of these responsorial psalms
after the first reading, but the Roman Gradual offers another
possible chant, the gradual. In the case of the anniversary of
dedication, the words of the gradual are unique to this celebration, though inspired by Jacob's declaration after his dream in
Genesis 28:16-17: "This place was made by God; it is a priceless
mystery, something irreproachable. O God, whom the choir of
angels attends, hear the prayers of your servants." The lovely
chant, *Locus iste*, puts its longest melisma over the Latin word
for "choir." Anton Bruckner wrote a popular choral setting of
the antiphon in the nineteenth century.

The Simple Gradual offers yet another option. It proposes
the same responsorial psalm it recommends for Holy Family
Sunday, all the verses of Psalm 84. It evidences the loveliness
of God's dwelling place both in the church and in the home.

In the Roman Gradual the gospel acclamation is called
the alleluiatic verse. It offers five options. The first is "I bow
down toward your holy temple. I give thanks to your name"

(Ps 138:2), which the gradual also assigns to the Fourth Week in Ordinary Time. In this liturgy, it inspires people to practice ancient postures of worship in their own holy place.

The second option, "The house of the Lord is well set upon a firm rock," probably alludes to Matthew 16:18, where Jesus declares Peter the rock upon whom he will build the church. On an anniversary celebration, it reminds the community their building has lasted long because of the faith of generations past.

The third possibility, "O Lord, I love the house where you dwell, the place where your glory abides" (Ps 26:8), also appears in the gradual as a suggestion for the Common of Holy Men and Women. Here it summons the affection people have for their long-established church.

The fourth, "I rejoiced when they said to me, 'Let us go to the house of the Lord'" (Ps 122:1), is also the gradual's suggestion for the Second Week of Advent. Here it invites people to rejoice each time they enter their place of worship.

The gradual's final option, "Praise is due to you in Sion, O God. To you we pay our vows in Jerusalem" (Ps 65:2), reappears for the Fifteenth Week in Ordinary Time. Here it connects the building to the history of Jerusalem, while foreshadowing the heavenly Jerusalem.

If the anniversary falls during Lent, the Roman Gradual offers a tract for the occasion, "Those who put their trust in the LORD are like Mount Sion, that cannot be shaken, that stands forever. Jerusalem! The mountains surround her; so the LORD surrounds his people, both now and forever" (Ps 125:1-2). It otherwise assigns this to the Fourth Sunday of Lent. Traditionally, the liturgy assigns the Mass for each day of Lent to one of the churches in the city of Rome, where pilgrims gather for worship. The station for the Fourth Sunday of Lent is the Basilica of the Holy Cross in Jerusalem, which houses relics of the passion, including wood from the cross of Christ. The tract, therefore, connects the anniversary of a church's dedication to the city of the ancient temple and of the sacrifice of Christ.

The Simple Gradual recommends only Psalm 122, either its two opening verses as the alleluia, or its entirety as the alleluiatic psalm.

Commentary on the second readings, the alleluia verse or verse before the gospel, and the gospel (Lectionary 704–706) is found in the treatment of Chapter II:54 above.

Offertory

Although no offertory antiphon appears in the Roman Missal, the Roman Gradual provides one for each Mass. It offers four possibilities for the anniversary of the dedication of a church.

The first is 1 Chronicles 29:17, 18, the same offertory recommended for the dedication of the church (ODCA II:72). King David spoke these verses as he offered his precious treasures to the temple shortly before his death. At the preparation of the gifts of the anniversary Mass, the community receives inspiration by David's act of generous giving. The ODCA offers an English translation with a much-simplified version of the notes from the Latin chant. The Roman Gradual also recommends it for the day of consecration of virgins and at the profession of religious. These dedicated men and women also imitate David in offering all to the Lord's dwelling place.

The second option comes from Daniel 9:4, (2,) 17, 19. The prophet prays that God will shine his face upon his sanctuary and show kindness to the people who call upon his name. Those who sing this on the anniversary of the dedication of their church demonstrate that they are among those calling upon God's name in a sanctuary, in hopes of receiving the Lord's kindness. This chant reappears as the Roman Gradual's offertory for the Twenty-Third Sunday in Ordinary Time.

Exodus 24:4, 5 provides the third option for the offertory. This passage records Moses's offering of an evening sacrifice upon an altar, sending a pleasing aroma to the attention of the Lord God. This verse is especially fitting for an evening anniversary Mass at which the celebrant takes the option to incense the gifts of bread and wine, the altar and the cross. The chant also appears in the Roman Gradual as the offertory for the Twenty-Fifth Sunday in Ordinary Time.

The fourth option concludes with an alleluia and therefore may not be used during Lent. Coming from Revelation 8:3, 4, it tells of the angel with a golden censer before the altar of the Lord, a passage much referenced in the ODCA. It is especially appropriate at anniversary Masses when the celebrant opts to use incense. The same chant appears in the celebration of the archangels Michael, Gabriel, and Raphael on September 29.

The Simple Gradual offers but one option for the offertory. It is the same text that the Roman Gradual lists as one possibility for the alleluiatic verse: "The house of the Lord is well set upon a firm rock." Again, this probably alludes to Matthew 16:18, where Jesus declares Peter the rock upon whom he will build the church. The Simple Gradual pairs this antiphon with Psalm 138, which pledges praise of God in the holy place in the sight of the angels. Again, if incense is used at the preparation of the gifts, this psalm resonates with the vision of the angel and the golden censer in Revelation 8:3-4.

Prayer over the Offerings

The prayer over the offerings for the anniversary Mass is a new composition that replaces the one from the preconciliar Missal: "Draw near to our prayers, O Lord, we pray, that those of us who celebrate its dedication anniversary day inside this temple may please you with full and perfect devotion of body and soul, so that, as we offer these present prayers, we may, by your help, be made worthy to arrive at eternal rewards. Through our Lord Jesus Christ, your Son, who lives and reigns with you in the unity [of the Holy Spirit for ever and ever]."

Now the prayer recalls the day when God filled this house "with glory and holiness," and asks that the Lord "may make of us a sacrificial offering always acceptable to you."

The new prayer expresses many sentiments of the revised rites. It probably alludes to Ezekiel 43:5, where the Spirit lifted the prophet up into the inner court of the temple, which the glory of the Lord then filled. As glory returned to the temple in Jerusalem, so God's glory has filled this dedicated church.

The intention that the people may become a sacrifice always acceptable to God also resounds in Eucharistic Prayer III (Order of Mass 113). It recalls St. Paul's appeal to the Romans to present their bodies as a living, acceptable sacrifice to God (Rom 12:1). The people who worship in this church are not just watching the sacrifice of the Mass; they offer themselves in sacrifice as well.

Preface

The preface for this Mass is the same one used in The Order of the Dedication of a Church in Which Sacred Celebrations Are Already Regularly Taking Place (ODCA III:35). A commentary can be found in Chapter III above.

Communion Antiphon

The antiphon recommended for communion is based on 1 Corinthians 3:16-17. "You are the temple of God, and the Spirit of God dwells in you. The temple of God, which you are, is holy." In Easter Time, the antiphon concludes with an alleluia. Newly added to the Missal after the council, this antiphon helps the people who receive communion to meditate on the sacredness of their bond with one another and with God.

The Roman Gradual suggests seven different options for the communion antiphon. It repeats the one from the preconciliar Missal: "My house shall be a house of prayer, says the Lord: in that house, everyone who asks receives, and the one who seeks finds, and to the one who knocks, the door will be opened." This is also the first of the suggested communion antiphons in The Order of the Dedication of a Church (ODCA II:78). A commentary can be found in Chapter II above.

On the anniversary, however, that refrain is paired not with Psalm 128 as in the dedication, but with a psalm of pilgrimage that opens with a meditation on the loveliness of God's dwelling place (Ps 84:2-3a, 3b, 4, 5, 9, 10, 11). All the other antiphons proposed by the gradual come with the same psalm verses. Whereas Psalm 128 proposes the image of the parish family gathered at the table of the Lord, Psalm 84 focuses more on the building, the object of the anniversary celebration.

The Roman Gradual suggests these alternatives: "You will delight in right sacrifice, burnt offerings wholly consumed, on your altar" (Ps 51:21), which the gradual also proposes as the communion antiphon for the Sixteenth Sunday in Ordinary Time. Here it connects the altar of eucharistic sacrifice with altars of old.

Or "Jerusalem is built as a city bonded as one together. It is there that the tribes go up, the tribes of the Lord, to praise the name of the Lord" (Ps 122:3-4). Both the gradual and the Missal also assign this to the Fourth Sunday of Lent, the day that the stational church in Rome is the Basilica of the Holy Cross in Jerusalem. It recalls the city of the Temple and of the cross of Christ, while anticipating the heavenly Jerusalem.

Or "I will come to the altar of God, to God who restores the joy of my youth" (Ps 43:4). The Missal also places this as the entrance antiphon for the Ritual Mass For the Dedication of an Altar, and the Roman Gradual places it on the Fifth Week in Ordinary Time. It repositions a verse from the psalms in the context of the people gathered at the altar of the dedicated church.

Or "The sparrow finds a home, and the swallow a nest for her young: by your altars, O Lord of hosts, my King and my God. Blessed are they who dwell in your house, for ever singing your praise" (Ps 84:4, 5). Both the Missal and the gradual also assign this to the Fifteenth Week in Ordinary Time. Here, as the people receive communion, they draw near to the altar of God as those who approached Jerusalem's Temple of old.

Or "Bring an offering and enter his courts; worship the Lord in holy splendor" (Ps 96:8, 9). The Roman Gradual also proposes this for communion of the Twenty-Fourth Week in Ordinary Time. As the people have entered this church many times and offered their lives at Mass, so they worship in a splendid anniversary celebration by receiving communion within the sacred place.

Or "There is one thing I ask of the Lord, only this do I seek: to live in the house of the Lord all the days of my life" (Ps 27:4). Both the Missal and the Roman Gradual also place this on the Eleventh Week in Ordinary Time. In this ceremony, as the people within the church draw near to the altar for communion, they delight to be inside the Lord's house, a place that foreshadows where they hope to live forever.

The Simple Gradual proposes only an abbreviated version of the traditional antiphon from Matthew: "My house shall be a house of prayer, says the Lord." It pairs with Psalm 147, which summons Jerusalem to praise God, who "has strengthened the bars of your gates" and "gives you your fill of finest wheat" (Ps 147:13-14).

These resources offer a rich selection of options from which the parish may choose to enhance its anniversary celebration. The biblical references are nearly inexhaustible, allowing for a deeper meditation on the meaning of their dedicated church, year by year.

The Titular Solemnity

The day when the calendar observes the saint or devotion associated with the Title of the church becomes a solemnity for the parish each year. Proper texts for the readings, antiphons, and prayers vary from one church to another. Still, those who prepare the liturgical celebration of the day should plan accordingly.

Usually, the date associated with the Title is well known. For lesser known saints, questions can be resolved through consulting the Roman Martyrology, the Vatican's book that assigns every saint to a day in the calendar.

In many instances, those who prepare the liturgy will need to consult the appropriate section of the Commons of the Saints in the Roman Missal and in the Lectionary for Mass. These provide a selection of options for antiphons, readings, and presidential prayers.

In the Missal, the commons contain the groups of relative antiphons and presidential prayers for a Mass that lacks them in the preceding section, the Proper of Saints. Some saints' days come with a proper collect but nothing more. The saints without a day on the general calendar do not even have their own collect. Their names are then inserted into a collect taken from the appropriate section of the commons, whether they are martyrs, pastors, or virgins, for example.

A large section of the commons provides Masses of the Blessed Virgin Mary. These demonstrate the widespread devotions that have created a large body of prayers over the centuries. If the parish church is dedicated to Mary, the community will likely find an appropriate Mass within this section. Alternatively, it may find the right choice in a separate publication, the Collection of Masses of the Blessed Virgin Mary, which contains dozens of celebrations in two volumes, one a Missal, the other a lectionary.

As a solemnity, the liturgy of the titular solemnity resembles a Sunday Mass. It includes the Gloria and the Creed, as well as three readings. It would be appropriate to conclude with a solemn blessing.

As with the dedication anniversary, the titular day provides an occasion for social celebration as well: a gathering of the parish community to enjoy one another's company, an invitation to neighbors to tour the church and the grounds.

After meditating on the charisms of the titular saint or the reasons for the titular devotion, the community may feel inspired to perform some act of service that made their patron holy in the eyes of the church. Such activities can put the faith that celebrates the liturgy into action in the community.

The observance of these two parish solemnities shows the lasting influence of the church's founders. They dreamed of a building and sacrificed their possessions for its construction, even as King David had done. They gathered the skills of artisans to make their place of worship a reality, as King Solomon had done. They sang songs of praise at its dedication, repeating the pilgrimage psalms of the men and women who first worshiped at the Jerusalem Temple.

The generation that takes part in the planning and celebration of a new church will create a building that lasts. That church will be a house where the glory of God dwells, a place where future believers will offer a pure sacrifice from the rising of the sun to its setting. The construction of a new church is exciting to witness. The people who behold the process and take part in the building's inauguration cannot imagine how many future generations will gather to remember their work of faith on two occasions each year: the titular solemnity of the new church, and the anniversary of its dedication. Future believers will do this because of some generous and generative community that once gave birth to a new church and a new altar.